D1132820

The Ripple Effect

Invisible Impact of Suicide

The Ripple Effect

For Garrett,

A book to remember Garrett, help others,
and encourage hope, love and communication.

We Love You, Garrett

Contents

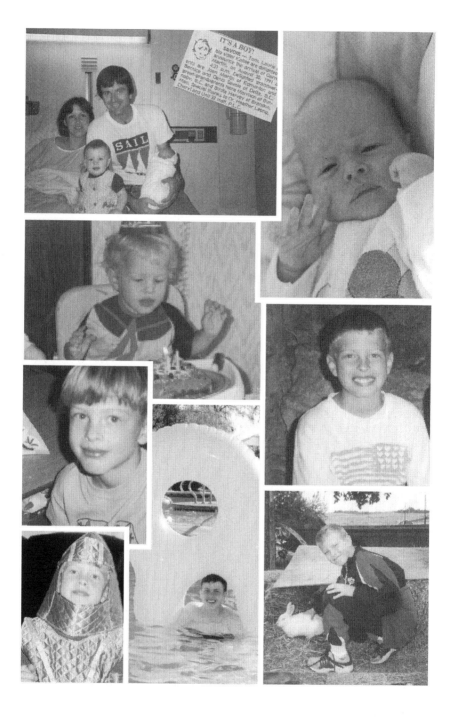

Garrett Martin Savoie

Garrett Martin Savoie

Garrett was born in Calgary, Canada on August 30, 1991, the only son of Tom and Laurie Savoie, and the grandson of Walter and Joan Martin of Edmonton and Denis and Bernice Savoie of White Rock. Garrett was blessed with a big sister, Kailee, and a little sister, Chantal, as well as many aunts, uncles, cousins and friends. He loved being around all of them, chatting, joking, playing sports, video games, and later in life, having a few beers with them.

Garrett moved to the U.S. with his family in 1998 and was excited to become a U.S. Citizen but he was very proud of his Canadian heritage. He started attending school in the Cave Creek School District and continued there until he graduated in 2009. He played soccer while he lived in Calgary, then started playing baseball and hockey after moving to the U.S. Hockey soon became his favorite sport until he was in middle school and experienced numerous injuries. Soon, paintball became his passion which he enjoyed until the day he passed away.

The entire family loved to travel. They took amazing family vacations as well as spent time visiting friends and family in Canada often. Garrett was part of a very large extended family that loved to spend time together, especially the annual summer vacations with his cousins in Calgary and Vancouver. During the summer of 2009, the family went on their last vacation to Mount Rushmore and Little Big Horn. Garrett especially loved this trip as he had a true passion for history.

Under Garrett's beaming smile, friendly and kind nature, he was in despair. He could not see the wonderful future he had ahead of him that all his friends and family could see so clearly for him. He is at peace now and we are so grateful that we had Garrett for 19 years; he gave us such joy for which we will be forever grateful.

Garrett, we miss you terribly. We love you more than you can imagine and we know that God and your grandparents have welcomed you with open arms as we know you will one day do for us. We love you forever!

Dear Readers,

I bring you this book with a heavy heart, but hopefully also HOPE. I know that all the caring people who contributed, to what I pray will be an inspiring book, have also experienced a heavy, sad heart, but my hope is that they also received some type of cathartic healing and a lightened heart.

My dream and desire in writing this book is that the contributors, as well as you the reader, will now see your lives through different eyes -- to enjoy *every* moment, hug someone, talk to a stranger, do a "pay it forward" with no expectations or thanks, contribute to a charity, or just a simple gesture--smile at someone!

By seeing and living each moment differently, you might have just changed someone else's minute, their future, their destiny -- by a simple act of caring and showing them: "They are worth it!!" Blessed moments to all who read this.

With much love,

Laurie

A message from Laurie

Dear Readers,

Many people have asked how this book came about. It was Thursday, May 15, 2013 at 5:40 PM and I was pulling out of our garage to go pick up my daughter, Chantal. I saw a figure, tall, thin and dressed all in black, behind the truck. It was my late son Garrett's spirit and he said to me, "C'mon Mom, I'm all ready to go on Oprah!"

You see, my beloved son Garrett took his own life on November 17, 2010 at the age of 19.

In my head I heard, "You should write a book about Garrett—how his suicide impacted people."

I have been shown and can clearly see this book in my head. I see it in 27 different countries and it hasn't even been written yet! This book is written from the other angle, to see what people left behind feel, and to see each person's value. It is intended to help young people or adults who are contemplating suicide, who are sad, depressed, suffering in silence. It is to be given to students in high schools, teen groups, and doctors' offices.

When I first received the message and then saw Garrett's book, I immediately tell myself and God, "No, no, no way, absolutely not!!" Well, for the next ten days or so, the image and messages kept getting louder and louder.

Unsure what to do, I talked to my therapist and life-coach Kim about this book, as at this point I was feeling more terrified than excited about the idea. As soon as I shared my vision and message with Kim, she became very excited, especially as she has personally experienced suicide in her own family, as well as supporting her clients who have lost a loved one, like myself. We both agreed we didn't think there was anything else out there like this. I left her office with a greater sense of confidence realizing that I had been given a divine message – to share the ripple effects of suicide.

To begin, I had to clear it with my family first. My husband's first reaction was "you don't know anything about writing, publishing, etc." I replied, "I'm not worried, it is coming directly to me from God/Divine, so I have faith that they will provide the right people each step of the way."

Once I made the commitment to do this, I sent out many letters to people we knew because I wanted to reach out to them personally and give them a physical piece of paper.

While I was photocopying the letter, a girl at the store said, "Suicide impacted my family from my sister's boyfriend, and I knew Garrett. Can I have some letters to pass out too?" I saw this as an immediate "gift", a validation regarding the mission of this book and suicide's ripple effect.

My friend Laura who I worked with didn't know Garrett, but wanted to contribute. Knowing she is an artist, I asked her if she would draw a picture. Well, with the help of her husband, John, Laura captured Garrett perfectly, and even suggested a book title, The Ripple Effect. Her story is included in this book, as I had no idea that her husband's mother had committed suicide as well as Laura's own good friend? Suicide affects many.

This book became exactly what I wanted it to be, a tapestry of feelings and stories about impact, the silent impact that is left behind after a suicide.

Death on the whole isn't talked about much, or well, and I can tell you from experience that the topic of suicide is a tough one. It is one thing to lose a child to an accident or disease, but it's an entirely different matter to lose a child by his or her own hand. In the former situation, parents suffer but don't question if they were a good parent. On the other hand, I have to carry the shameful burden of, "Why??? Wasn't I a good enough parent?"

Suicide—what do you say to someone when they ask how your child died? When *you* don't even really know why? Mixed with the devastating sadness, I had to work through guilt and the stigma of "not good enough Mother syndrome" I created for myself.

What I would love to see come out of this book is Love, Communication and Hope.

Love, because for me it all comes down to love: love yourself, your family, and others. Everyone wants to love and be loved.

Communication is another critical key. We tried so many things for Garrett, but he never really told us how he was feeling and he was never a good communicator. Boys typically seem to hold things, words, emotions in, and if this book can change the way one boy communicates, then I'll be truly happy.

Hope, so that if you are down, you can see that you are worthy.

Hope for those left behind after suicide to let you know that you are not alone and can truly survive it.

I also want to share some of my experiences from this awful, life-changing act that may help you or others:

• This is a club no one wants to belong to.

• Don't bring any live plants to care for. I could barely breathe let alone look after another living thing.

• Eating, sleeping, normal behavior just doesn't happen—I must have walked 10 miles in my house and never went anywhere, lost 10 lbs, and didn't sleep for 10 days.

• I was in a cocoon state for about two years, and my memory is gone from that time period.

• Just be on the survival plan: one second, get through the next second, and the next…

I could offer many more pointers to assist in how to survive, and find ones new normal. However, I don't want this to be a grief book.

I pray that this book will be helpful for those left behind, and for anyone contemplating suicide. In reading this book, you will see how many lives Garrett touched, and how significant each person is – even if you are currently questioning this truth. I hope each of you will think about your worth here on Earth, and how important it is for YOU to be ALIVE!

Blessed moments to all who read this.

With much love,

Laurie

Forward

I've had a couple of friends who have lost a loved one to suicide over the past couple of years. It was a time of sudden and unexpected shock and trauma. As I supported them through their journey of loss I noticed the grief process was more challenging than was the case with a natural death.

I did some research into the topic and discovered several reasons for the unique complications to the bereavement process resulting from suicide. Some were tied to the feelings of guilt survivors had, others were related to the mental health stigma, and some to the sudden and unexpected nature of the end. These are all valid yet they lay in the basket of silence that is the most difficult challenge to overcome.

The cone of silence placed around suicide is what complicates survivor's emotional healing the most. It is what causes a unique and hushed grief - from my perspective the toughest grief to suffer through. No one knows what to say, what to do, or how to support those grieving the loss of a loved one who took their own life. There are myths and beliefs many people hold around suicide that hinder the natural unfolding of grief in the warm arms and hearts of family, friends, and community.

I applaud Laurie's efforts to shine the light of day on this maligned and misunderstood taboo topic of suicide. The way to heal these tragic and all too common deaths is to talk about them fully, publicly, and unabashedly; to talk about suicide with courage, compassion, and care; To let people know there is life after suicide and the aching grief associated with it; To let people know there is a warm heart and attentive listening available.

This book is a community built work of art.

Stephen Garrett, author of *When Death Speaks: Listen, Learn and Love*

When Laurie first shared with me the concept of Garrett's book, I immediately knew at a deep level that "YES! Our world needs this book." Learning that *"The Ripple Effect, Invisible Impact of Suicide"* was inspired by a divine message further strengthened my conviction.

Since then I have had the honor of helping Laurie persevere through the emotional and logistical challenges of writing this book. I admire the strength, courage and determination it has taken for Laurie and her family to re-open the heartbreaking loss of Garrett, and all the raw emotions surrounding his choice and its reverberating impact.

Having personally and professionally experienced the ripple effect of suicide over the past 30 years, I know that processing a suicide is different from most other losses. It's an emotional rollercoaster, starting with Elizabeth Kübler-Ross's initial five stages of grief. But grieving a suicide is much more complicated and includes feelings of guilt, confusion, turmoil, shame, blame and remorse.

The first suicide I personally experienced was when my beloved young cousin, who was a very sweet and considerate, straight-A student, took his own life at the tender age of twelve. He made this rash decision because he was despondent over the loss of his first love. Unfortunately for him, and for so many others who make this desperate decision, he was too young to know that the deep pain he felt - literally like his heart was breaking - would subside. Most children, teenagers, and adults who choose to end their lives, are really only wanting their pain to end. A powerful acronym I often share to address this despair is, **HOPE: Hold On Pain Ends.**

Sadly, the number of suicides is increasing, unlike other deaths. Therefore, when we see people struggling with depression and hopelessness, it is vital to take them seriously. According to the Jason Foundation Parent Resource Program, suicide is the SECOND leading cause of death for ages 10-24, and is the THIRD leading cause of death for college-age youth and ages 12-18. More teenagers and young adults die from suicide than from cancer, heart disease, AIDS, birth defects, stroke, pneumonia, influenza, and chronic lung disease, COMBINED.[1] Additionally, the American Foundation for Suicide Prevention reports that suicide is now the 10th leading cause of death in our nation, and more males commit suicide by 4 to 1. "From 1999 to 2010, the suicide rate among Americans ages 35 to 64 rose by nearly 30 percent."[2]

Fortunately, wonderful resources like the National Suicide Prevention Lifeline and Suicide Prevention Centers now exist for those who need help. Additionally, there are national support groups like Survivors of Suicide (SOS), which weren't available three decades ago when my family experienced this devastation. Suicide is still not openly discussed like other types of loss. But with information like this much-needed book, awareness spreads and helps to give a voice, education and resources to what was once a silent grief.

Those who contributed to this meaningful book were all affected by Garrett's choice and motivated to help others by sharing their heartfelt words of encouragement to let others know they are not alone, and to hopefully provide new, conscious choices.

Laurie and I envision "The Ripple Effect, Invisible Impact of Suicide" being available in therapists' and doctors' offices, schools and libraries, for anyone who wants to learn more and/or comfort someone in need. We hope this book will create its own ripple effect of healing, by providing an inspiring and transformative perspective on the importance of life. Each person does matter – you matter.

Kim Evans
Transformational Coach
Your Wings

"We ourselves feel that what we are doing is just a drop in the ocean. But the ocean would be less because of that missing drop." *Mother Teresa*

[1] http://jasonfoundation.com/prp/facts/youth-suicide-statistics/

[2] The New York Times, May 2nd, 2013 by Tara Parker-Pope, http://www.nytimes.com/2013/05/03/health/suicide-rate-rises-sharply-in-us.html?_r=0

*More resources on pages 256-257

The letter for submissions

I am writing to you today, because our family is embarking on a new, and what we envision as being a meaningful book project -- and if you feel comfortable participating, we would greatly appreciate your support. As you know, our family experienced the tragic loss of our beloved Garrett Martin. Since that day on November 17, 2010, as a family and individually, we have been striving to heal and move forward. I personally still find myself from time to time wondering 'why'… knowing we will never really know.

Throughout the last 2 3/4 years, what I have learned is that Garrett's death affected more people than his own and our family's inner circle. Friends of friends and others that Garrett didn't even know have felt the ripple suicide creates. So many lives have been touched and forever changed by Garrett's choice, and with the passage of time and healing, we would now like to create what we hope will provide a positive ripple of support, understanding and healing.

Our family's vision is to compile a book that will include thoughts, reflections, reactions, poems, songs, drawings, etc. – anything that you would like to share that has emerged for you surrounding Garrett's choice and passing.

Recently, I received a vision that a book compiled of everyone's thoughts, feelings and experiences, which were touched and/or affected by Garrett's death, may help someone considering suicide make a different choice. Additionally, for those that are left behind, we hope this book will provide them comfort, knowing they are not alone. Plus, they will be able to read how others felt, and dealt with this sudden loss, and any positive and/or healing ripples that may have occurred.

If you feel moved to contribute to what we hope will be a life-changing book, we would love your input. I realize for some, what I'm asking may be too much, just too emotional, so please don't feel pushed. For those that feel comfortable participating and want to help, the following are some guidelines (don't feel obligated to answer any or all of the below). Anything you would like to share is welcome and appreciated:

• How did you know Garrett and/or our family or are you a friend of a friend, etc.?

• Where were you when you first heard about Garrett's suicide?

• What was your first reaction when you first heard the news?

• What did you think – disbelief, surprised, not surprised, etc., and have your thoughts changed over time?

• What did you feel or were you in shock, numb, etc. and have your feelings changed over time?

• How has this changed, impacted and/or touched your heart, life and those in your life?

• Do you know others that didn't know Garrett but have been impacted by you sharing your feelings and experience?

Please know that we don't have a particular format in mind, and feel free to contact me with any questions you may have. As I shared, we welcome photos, poetry, song lyrics, even a letter you wrote or now want to write to Garrett - whatever comes naturally to you. If you feel moved to use hard language, that's how you felt...and it will be included in your writing.

Again I want to express and underline that we realize this may be a very emotional exercise to ask of anyone, so we support anyone's choice to not participate. For those that want to contribute, please know that our family's mission in writing this book is to help save lives and let someone know how truly special they are ALIVE!

We envision this book in therapist and doctors' offices, schools, libraries, and anyone's home who has the desire to lift and change someone's life and behavior. Each one of us, sharing our own feelings and thoughts are offering the world a message, which may inspire hope and new, conscious choices. We hope this book will create a healing ripple...as we believe your heartfelt words have the ability to 'gift' someone with a new and a potentially inspiring and life-changing perspective...

If you are willing to share, please do so.

Please feel free to pass this onto anyone we may not know about, or contact me to send this out to someone for you. Again many thanks, and God bless you!

With much love and gratitude,

Laurie and the Savoie Family

Tom, Kailee and Chantal

Dear mom,

I love you so much! I never meant to cause you the pain that I did. I know that you love me as much as a ~~mom~~ mother can love her son. That look you gave me on wednesday before Part 1 is permanetly ~~engraved~~ in my head. I can't picture your face without crying It pains me so much. I never wanted to disrupt how our family ~~operates~~ operates. Now that the majority of my ~~former~~ friends have left me I realize how much my family truly means to me.

Written by Garrett
February, 2008

Section One: **FAMILY**

Family is one of the most precious things that a person can have in this world. For the most part, they are the ones who know you best and can share some of your very earliest memories. In this section, Garrett's relatives offer how they felt and still feel about the impact that his suicide created in their lives. Together, they share beautiful memories, an overwhelming sense of loss, and a collective focus on trying to make sense of a tragedy such as this. Every emotion possible is found in these words and it's important for readers to realize that suicide touches everyone in a very individual way. This section highlights the devastating process that a family goes through as they try to cope and continue living without an important piece of their family.

November 21, 2010 – The speech Laurie gave at Garrett's Memorial:

Thanks so much for coming today to honour my beautiful son, Garrett Martin.

Garrett came into this world looking like an old man, but he was always young at heart with a gentle soul. He was a handful from day one, full of energy. He always kept us hopping.

We struggled this past year or longer trying to get him healthy and off of drugs. We had our precious son back for three glorious months until two weeks ago when he withdrew from us.

Let me tell you about my beloved son, Garrett. He had ADHD and didn't sleep through the night until 2 years, 4 months old. He didn't eat food until the summer he was turning 5. He lived on air and sunshine.

He was really young when his Uncle Rick nicknamed him GMAN and his sister LADY K.

He was always shy and quiet but, with a great sense of humour. He had a beautiful beaming smile and a gentle nature.

He loved being busy and was always going, going. He played soccer, baseball and tons and tons of street and ice hockey.

He was proud to be Canadian and loved to travel there to see his aunts, uncles and many cousins. He loved all of our family reunions, playing crib, war movies, history, and the Guinness Book of World Records.

He loved movies, paintballing, boating, animals, his friends, his sisters, us--he loved his family.

I will never forget all the times he said to me, even at 19 years old, "C'mon Mom, are you up for a hot tub?"

He loved being home, playing his video and computer games, watching movies. He loved cooking with me when he was young. He loved my cooking, especially my Greek salad.

He loved working at his Auntie Barbie's and Uncle Glenn's restaurants. His two favorite restaurants were Jalapenos and The Keg.

He was reliable, trustworthy, he was there when you needed him. He was respectful, mannerly and didn't want to disappoint us.

He had recently got a job with Jason at Jason's nursery and landscaping company which he truly loved. He was so proud to show me all around the nursery and he loved working outside with his hands.

I am a strong person, Garrett, and I will make something good come out of this. I promise you.

We were always so proud of you, Garrett, and you know you were always loved.

I miss you GMAN, look out for us from heaven. XXXXOOOOXXXOOO

Chicks in the nest, BE safe, I LOVE YOU.

August 29, 2013 Thursday

My dearest Garrett,

It is one day before your birthday. Tomorrow we should be celebrating your 22nd birthday. Instead, I am asking people to write about how your suicide has affected them in hopes of now helping other people. This is so wrong, sickening, twisted. I haven't even been able to read the stuff people have submitted already. It is still so raw.

Apparently, I am finding out from my counselor, Kim, that my whole life - since I was a little kid - I have zoomed right though all of the yucky stuff so I didn't have to deal with it. Glossed over it, pretended it didn't happen. Possibly, so I didn't have to feel the pain. Things like my dad dying suddenly at the age 55, when I was 24 years old, and when my Mom got cancer and died at the age of 66--I always appeared strong and together. I had the mentality that said, "I'm tough, I can handle it." I appeared to soldier on with a positive outlook and a smile.

I feel *so* sad as I write this. Oh, what a strong bond you and I shared! I will love you to the end of time (even though you were an incredible amount of work from the minute you came to earth). After you passed away, your Dad said to me, "Why was he *so* much work for 19 years?" I told him, "Why did God think we were *so* amazing that we could handle it?"

We all tried to help you feel good your whole life. Even right up to the very end. Even phoning you that day. I know you heard our calls. I know you hated disappointing us. Well, Garrett, *this* is a disappointment that cannot be changed or reversed.

I have looked back with many "shoulda, woulda, coulda's", but deep down I know I did the best I could--*always*. I might not be Mother-of-the-Year but you *knew* you were, and are, loved. I wish I had listened more, paid attention to see if there were any signs or indications this was a possibility for you. Even then, I doubt I would have seen anything.

You were always so impulsive, not tuned in to the consequences. At nine years old I still had to tell you to watch for cars on the street! I'm sure your choice the morning of November 17th was not thought out.

Sometimes I want to run away, move away, get out of this situation our family is now forced into coping and living with, and then I realize it's pointless. How do you run away from what's going on inside your own head?

Your "little" sister for the past two years or so, out of the blue will totally sound like you or have an expression you did. At first, I thought you were channeling through her, but then I realized you are both just so similar. I don't want to point it out to her because it is like a gift--like having you back again on earth. She worries me though because she is the same as you - quiet, won't share her emotions or how she is feeling. No wonder you guys would fight, you were so similar.

I worry about your sister, Kailee. You two were so close. She tried and tried to help you feel better, to check if things were okay. At least you had her to talk to. She is probably going to end up on a life mission, a career, to help others feel good about themselves.

We are all changed and I'm not even sure it's for the better. I have walls up now. My free spirit is partly beaten down. I can hardly even bear to hug your sisters for fear of getting too close and losing them, too. It's so sad.

What I do know is:

You didn't think about all of your friends and how this would impact them, how they would miss you, and how they would wish things were different. Or how this would impact your extended family or all the people you worked with, played sports with . . .

You didn't think about your little seven-year-old cousin, Josh, who adored you. You were his favorite cousin. How your actions ripped him off by not having you around for the rest of his life. How he looked up to you, loved hanging with you and how you could have been so great in his life.

I feel ripped off that you won't be here with a wife or grandkids for me. Everyone who knew you knew how amazing you were with little kids. The kids at all the summer camps, vacation bible school and the after-school-kids-club all adored you.

I still can't take your room apart yet and that tells me that I truly don't believe that you're gone off this earth.

You have changed our family dynamic. We all miss your energy, your sense of humor, your playfulness. Man, you could get us all laughing! Our family *and* the world is ripped off!

I *know* you came on earth to teach your dad and I unconditional love.

I wish:

I had listened more. I wish you had talked more, too. I wish I had hugged you more. You gave amazing hugs.

I loved that you liked to stay home even when you were older. I now think you picked up what other people were feeling and thinking and it was safe at home. I get it, I feel the same. I wish you had talked to me, told me how you were feeling. Maybe I could have helped you.

I hadn't found out you were using drugs until after you were 18. Then, I couldn't help you, force you to go somewhere away from it all because you were an adult. What I do think is that the drugs slowed your brain down and you felt good for the first time in your life. Your ADHD was under control.

I wish one of the many things we offered to you to help you had actually helped. Or that we could have done more to show you that things would be okay – that *you* were okay – awesome – great.

I miss watching *Wipe Out* with you and all the funny TV shows that you watched. Now, I see your sister watching all of the same shows you liked: history shows, reality shows about whale watching, and fishing. I miss you having your friends over playing video games, air soft, paintball, or watching movies.

I remember you coming home from the movie theatre all excited. "Mom, I just found your new favorite movie, Freedom Writers!!" It was all about a teacher who saw the potential in everyone and made them the best people they could be even though they had so much against them. That did become my favorite movie because I feel exactly like that teacher, always seeing the best in everyone and letting them know it. How I wish you could have seen yourself through my eyes.

I *so* miss your gorgeous smile, beautiful eyes, great hugs, hilarious jokes and sense of humor, our hot tub talks, and crib games. I remember driving by you on your way to work at the nursery and you saw me and flashed me your beautiful happy smile and your gentle wave. Such a simple gesture, now a treasured memory in my mind.

I always said I was on earth to make people feel good and to look after God's animals. My hope is that others, especially boys, will feel their worth and that they will learn to talk and share and not to keep things in. I hope that this book does exactly that--make people *know* and *feel* how amazing and special they are and to reach out for help if they need it. If this book changes one person's attitude then maybe it will be worth it.

I don't have to tell you how very much I love you because you know that. You felt that from me hopefully always. Now I'm hoping that something good will come out of our sadness.

With SOOOO much love for you Garrett,

Mom XXXXXXXXXXXXXXXXXXXXXXXXXXXOOOOOOOOOOOOOOOOOOOOO

Laurie and Garrett

2008

Hahahah!!! I thought this would make you laugh. Happy 45th Birthday. I hope it's a good one! Thanks for everything you have done for me.

Happy Birthday old timer!

LOVE,

GARRETH

"Look at those dang fool teenagers, wearing their pants hangin' down low like a coupla idiots."

2009

Dear mom,

Kinda makes you want
to rethink that whole
"DON'T PLAY WITH YOUR FOOD"
thing, doesn't it?

HAPPY MOTHER'S DAY!

I love all that you have done
for me and you have no idea how great
my life is because you are in it. Thanks
for all that you have done. I love
you!

Love,
Garrett

Hi Laurie. I tried to think of the message Garrett would like to send to any young person whose demons are getting the better of them and so I wrote what I thought he'd want to say.

I don't have too thick of skin so you can tell me if it's too strong.

Love you,
Judy

Stick Around

They say when you hit rock bottom

There's only one way to go

And that's up

That may be true

But it sure feels like

You spend a helluva long time

At the bottom

How many days and weeks

Can you open your eyes?

And see only black

Feeling that same ole knife

Turning in your gut

Wondering if you have a pulse

You fake chilling

When you see your friends

Hey man, wazzup?

But you're really stretching it

To make it look real

Take the exit option

The little voice says

C'mon take it

Why suffer

I'll take all the pain away

I'm the ticket

Just do it

End it now

C'mon I dare you

What a frickin' trickster

Once you head out that exit door

There's no return ticket

It's over!

You get that?

O-V-E-R over.

Next year

When all your stuff'd be worked out

And let's face it, man

It ALWAYS gets worked out in the end

No way can we text you

Or bump into you

And say

Hey, wanna get a beer?

Wanna watch the game?

Wanna hang out?

We all got older and

Life got a whole lot better

But where are you?

You'd be so choked

To see what you're missing.

Dear Laurie,

Thank you for the letter you sent recently about the project of a book on Garrett. Here are a few answers to your questions.

1. We remember Garrett as a beautiful blond boy. His family visited us in Quebec City around 1998 with his mom and dad and sister, Kailee. Justin, our third and youngest son, born in March 1992, was about Garrett's age. We had a wonderful time together during summer. The children drew pictures and I think Garrett drew children diving in a pool. I couldn't find the drawing; the family probably kept it. The visit was, if I recall right, just after the Savoie's reunion at Ste-Adèle. We saw the extended family another time during the Savoie reunion in 2006 in the Ottawa area. Since 1998, the family had grown, Chantal was there. The boys were already teenagers.

2. We learned about Garrett's death while we were at home in Quebec City.

3. We were so surprised. Our son, Justin, had received a message from Garrett through Facebook just a few weeks before his death.

4. We couldn't understand, but we didn't have the details of what happened.

5. We felt so sorry for Garrett. He had probably made some mistakes, but all mistakes can be repaired. We were very sad for the family.

6. Raising kids is not an easy task, particularly in an open society like ours. Our Christian values are always threatened in our society. Our kids are invited so early to become consumers of cigarettes, alcohol, drugs, and sex as soon as they become teenagers. For parents, it is very difficult. Are parents and professors teaching children how to think and behave in a responsible way? One can get discouraged when watching T.V. or reading from the internet, there are so many traps. Our kids are living in a dangerous society. Here in Quebec, just to convey our Christian faith is a very difficult task.

But here in Quebec, there are things that are done for our kids that are very good. When they make one or a few mistakes, they receive help to correct the situation. We do not send them to jail. We spend more time on prevention or rehabilitation than on plain punishment. Dear Laurie and Tom, I have just read what our son Justin wrote and I was moved to hear him saying that the family was important, supporting each other was important and life was fragile and a precious gift. Let's take precious care of the children while they are with us, also taking care of relatives, friends and community while asking God to provide strength to travel through our journey on earth to become better human beings and to thank God for witnesses that show us his true love.

All my affection,

Christiane (and Philippe)

Laurie,

I've read your letter a couple of times. I've also read what my mom wrote before me. I wish I could add more to it, but it's hard for me to find the right words--the right thing to say. I remember some memories, especially in 2006, when I was 14, Garrett 15 I suppose, and we met in Ottawa along with the Makowski boys. It was a pleasant memory for me, hanging out with the boys. I remember especially the hotel where we had spent time. However, it's also far back, when I was 14, lots of things are more or less clear, you know, time passes. I had spent a very nice time on vacation with Garrett and Jason, who had a brother, if my memory is correct but whose name I forget.

Also, of course, there was that conversation I had on Facebook with him during the summer of 2010. Recently, I looked up on my history of conversations and didn't find anything. It could have brought back memories from what we said, from what he had confided to me. Honestly, I don't know why it wasn't possible for me anymore to see what we wrote together but I guess its fine like this, also. What I simply remember is him talking to me about how tough it had been during recent months and how he might have forthcoming problems with his probation agent or something like that (this part I'm really not sure, 2010 is far back). I remember myself telling him that he should just continue that he would find opportunities. I'm not so sure of that either. I know I had listened to him more than I had talked, but it was just a "keeping up". We hadn't spoken to each other in years. When I learned the news from my parents who received it from my grandmother, I was also shocked by it. It takes you by surprise. It's hard to understand when something like that happens.

Completely unrelated to that, I also have a very good friend of mine, Etienne. This is someone whom I knew since second grade who died at age 19 from a heart condition during a trip to Greece. Of course, the situation is different, but it's hard for me not to relate the two events. Two young adults, who each had a life to live, but who, unfortunately, were not granted this opportunity. It's more questions than answers, but for me just talking about it with my family and friends helped me. In the same line of events, writing these small paragraphs to you is not a lot, but I think it can possibly help all of us in conveying a message of hope (here as in many other places in the text I'm not sure it's the perfect way to say it). Some things happen that we can't always understand, but there is a path to follow maybe to realize that life is fragile, that we must take care of it and we should always realize it's a precious gift.

It's only a small message I send to you from a cousin who knew Garrett a little-- remembering few, but awesome moments spent together. Family is important, supporting each other is important and I hope you will continue in your project.

Justin

Laurie and Tom

I'm afraid that we won't be much help to you, but we do want to congratulate you for wanting to do something about it.

Teenage suicide is happening all too often. There must be something that we as parents are lacking because we are unable to communicate with our own children. It is a very difficult time for kids to grow up. The pressures on them from society are enormous. Sometimes, despite the encouragement from parents to share their problems and concerns, kids just find this too difficult. We really never knew Garrett, but we certainly know his parents and our hearts go out to you. We hope that by researching the circumstances surrounding Garrett's death that you will find peace of mind. We share your sorrow and wish you the best.

Sincerely,

Nora and Norm

Hi Laurie,

I wanted to let you know that we received your letter just the other day. Thank you for the work you and your family will be doing to create a book that, with no doubt, will touch somebody's life. I hope that through the process, you and your family may also feel some hope or therapy or something... it is so hard to know what to say. Death, especially suicide is so hard for people to talk about and I think your book may just help bring suicide out of the shadows.

I don't think I have too much that would be a suitable addition to your book. I know that when I heard about Garrett's death, I was shocked. Unfortunately, I didn't know him all that well. However, what I knew (or what I thought I knew) was that he seemed so... well, "together". He appeared happy and active and alive! It makes me wonder how many people put on the "face" of doing "ok" and are hiding a secret pain. It makes me sad to know that people are suffering alone and that there are so many other people who would more than willingly take on a share of the suffering for their loved one (or even a perfect stranger, for that matter).

Please let me know how I can further support you and your family in this endeavour (if at all). I wish you all the best and much, much love.

God Bless you,

Michelle

Hi Laurie,

Thank you for including us in honoring Garrett, by giving us this opportunity to contribute to his book. We truly appreciate the gesture.

Mine and Mike's best memory of Garrett is from the summer of 2000, when we had the opportunity to look after both Garrett and Chantal.

That summer was a sad time with your mom being ill and passing away. It is nice for us to have such a happy and fun memory to brighten that summer.

We took Garrett and Chantal to the park near your mom's which was within walking distance. It was a beautiful day and Mike and Garrett played soccer in the field, while Chantal, who was in her stroller, Beau and I watched the boys play. I had Beau on a leash and at one point he became so excited about another nearby dog that he wrapped himself around the stroller and myself. We were in the sandy area by the slides. I almost fell over trying to unwrap Beau and prevent the stroller from tipping over. I lost a shoe in the process and thankfully a nearby couple with their own toddler came over to assist.

Of course, Mike and Garrett saw the whole thing from the soccer field and were laughing their heads off!! Chantal was also smiling and enjoying the moment!!

After some time at the park, we walked back to your mom's where we had supper, watched some TV and played games. You came home and our shift was suddenly over. I bet Mike and I were in bed the earliest that night. We had forgotten how much energy children that age and a dog can have!

We had such a fun and enjoyable time that day. We have often reminisced about how much fun we had!

We remember Garrett as enjoying sports and having a wonderful sense of humor. He could make anyone laugh! He was fun, pleasant and full of energy! It was apparent that day that he loved his little sister and enjoyed spending time with her, unlike some boys that age who often like to ditch their younger sisters.

Although we hadn't seen Garrett on a regular basis, we felt like we really knew him and re-connected with him after spending that one day together! It was truly an honor knowing him and he will always remain in our thoughts and prayers!

Thank you again for this wonderful opportunity,

Kathy Martin-Currie and Michael Currie

To Garrett:

To the sweet little "cuz" of mine.

I knew you from the time that you were a little one. I knew you as a happy go lucky little scoundrel. I only really wish I was able to see you grow more as I could've let you know it's not as easy as they say it is, but that doesn't mean there's nowhere to turn. That also doesn't mean that you aren't here anymore. I know you are above, around and inside of us. I know you are still happy and go-lucky and still sweet. The only difference now is that we can't see you with our eyes and we can't hear you with our ears unless we pay attention, but that doesn't mean you are not still here. Whenever I feel sad that you are not right there, I'll just stop and think for one split second, pay attention Duncan, he's been here the whole time.

Duncan

Hi Laurie,

We received your letter for requests on thoughts. If you think you will receive Joe's thoughts, good luck. Men avoid talking about these things with great tenacity. Because we didn't get to know Garrett as closely as others did, I will speak in general terms.

Until I can give it my full attention and careful thought, here are my preliminary thoughts.

Many neuroscientists have been publishing their studies about the brain and a lot can be learned from reading the information documented by these scientists.

Taking one's own life is a product of depression. Depression makes a person unable to take on any stress in life. Depression makes them unable.

Thanks, And good luck, Doreen

I am Garrett's aunt, his dad Tom's older sister.

Garrett's dad is my youngest brother. I was 14 when he was born, so yes – he's my favourite brother!! Garrett had a very special place in my heart because he was a lovable, special kid, but also because he was Tom's son.

Garrett reminded me a lot of my own son John – bright, lovable, fun-loving, but with the Achilles heel of ADHD. Lots of poor choices were made by both these beautiful boys, mainly because of their ADHD, including messing around with drugs. My son won his war on drugs, but lost the one with alcohol. He died in a car crash 18 years ago. He was the driver and there were crushed beer cans on the dashboard in the wreck. I had such high hopes that Garrett was going to make better choices than John. The news of Garrett's death was devastating and doubly so because it felt like a replay of John's death. The pain and sadness of losing those boys, of never being able to hug them again, of not being able to watch their lives unfold, hits very hard. I asked myself over and over, *what could we have done to help them make better choices?* I know that ultimately their choices were their responsibility.

Being a teenager is terribly hard work--figuring out who you are, establishing yourself as your own person separate from your parents, finding out what you like to do for fun, starting to think about a career, building friendships and keeping yourself safe from harm. It's sometimes quite miserable and lonely dealing with all of that, especially when you think it isn't going well. Maybe we don't talk about this enough and especially about the fact that we *all* go through these miserably lonely times. For many of us, the teenage years were the worst years of our lives and when we were experiencing them, we thought we were the only ones having a miserable time. There is a lot of talk these days about conveying to gay teenagers the knowledge that "It gets better". I'd like *every* teenager to have an intense course in "it gets better" so they will know that if they just hang on, circumstances *will* change.

What I've learned from these great losses is that the only way out of the misery is to work through the pain and sadness. And what helps the most is to get and give hugs, to express love and to ask others for support. Support is out there. You give a wonderful gift to someone when you reach out to them and ask them to share their wisdom about what they did to survive their tough times. And I've found that it's usually the most unexpected people whose words can make the biggest difference. I love that country song *"Life's a dance you learn as you go, sometimes you lead and sometimes you follow"*. When you're in pain and misery, it's time to follow. Find people to ask for support. Be bold –we're out there just waiting to be asked.

Cathie Savoie

Hello Tom and Laurie,

Your letter has stirred so many emotions, provoked many discussions, and at the end of the day, we realized there are just not enough words to describe how sad we feel about Garrett and for you and your children. You are genuinely wonderful human beings and have positively impacted so many lives.

We knew Garrett as our rambunctious, mischievous and joyful nephew and cousin who loved playing video games and paintball. When Tom called Rick on that fateful day on November 17, 2010, it was hard to imagine that this young man so full of life and promise had taken his life. It was incomprehensible that just the year before we had attended Garrett's graduation. We were so excited and proud to be part of that momentous occasion. Never would we have thought that Garrett's life would spiral into such despair.

Later, we learned that he struggled with self-worth, and low self-esteem, and that he had been bullied. This is one of our greatest regrets--if only we had known how alone and isolated he must have felt. Statistically too many young people, especially young boys, are ending their lives. There must be more support systems in place for parents, teachers, and friends to recognize the symptoms of depression. Young people must understand the finality of their actions. There are avenues to turn to. There are other ways to process your fears and frustration. Life does not have to end.

If only we could have convinced Garrett that tomorrow is a new day--an awesome day--and this too shall pass. There are solutions and rewards. Believe that there is hope. Life is not always easy, but with strength and determination one can overcome. Believe that you have a talent, you are valued. According to Uncle Rick, the best therapy is to work with your hands, to work hard physically.

Garrett's action that fateful day was a very impulsive decision. Garrett knew that he was loved and he regretted the pain he caused his family. In that split second moment, he just didn't see a way out of his situation.

Someone once said that "suicide is the most sincere form of self-criticism."

Elaine & Rick

Garrett was my cousin's son and I didn't know him very well. I saw him every three years as our family had regular family reunions. It was good to see how he progressed over the years into a nice young man.

My first reaction to the news of Garrett's suicide was total shock and my heart went out to his parents and sisters. I always wished I lived closer to them so I could somehow help them in anyway. It breaks my heart to see how this tragedy has affected his family. Also, it is so sad to know that Garrett must have felt that he could not talk with someone who would have been able to help him through the trials that he was going through. It also makes me ask the question, *what makes people feel so down on themselves that they would take their own lives?* I also wonder why those people don't consider their family and friends that are left behind. There are so many questions that could be asked, but I guess they will never be answered. Hopefully, this book project will be able to help other people who are considering ending their life. Life is so precious and we should enjoy every moment.

Lynn Handregan

Dear Laurie, Tom, Kailee and Chantal,

I think what you are doing is such a wonderful thing. Thank you for including me. I think of you often and want to share a thought for you.

You have your memories, hold on tight for comfort.

Know you have your family and friends you can count on for strength.

Remember how much you are loved.

Jennifer mentioned this book would be one she would put in her office. Wishing you the best of everything and take care.

Love,

Anne

Good for you Laurie. All I can say in my case for Garrett, you can re-write or add the poem I sent you from First Nation American author, *The Apache Blessing.* Stay strong and happy Laurie and spread the joy in memory of Garrett.

Much love,

Cousin Monique xx

May the sun bring you new energy by day, may the moon softly restore you by night, may the rain wash away your worries, may the breeze blow new strength into your being, may you walk gently through the world and know its beauty all the days of your life.

Poem by unknown Native American author:

Don't stand by my grave and weep for I'm not there. I do not sleep. I'm a thousand winds that blow, I'm the diamond's glint on snow, I'm the sunlight on ripened grain, I'm the gentle autumn's rain. In the soft hush of the morning light I'm the swift bird in flight. Don't stand by my grave and cry, I'm not there. I did not die.

Love to you and Tom,

Cousin Monique xx

_____

The shock. The disbelief. The sadness. The anger. The confusion. These are just a smattering of the emotions you experience when someone you care deeply about makes a decision, whether it was made in a clear state of mind or not, to take their own life.

Although we lived in different countries the majority of our lives and were several years apart in age, the combination of shared blood and shared personalities made me feel much closer to my cousin, Garrett. The person who left me shocked, in disbelief, saddened, angry and confused.

When I think of Garrett I prefer to think about the happier times. When his contagious smile and mischievous nature could brighten anyone's day. Our families often expressed how similar our personalities were. We were both quite the troublemakers as children, always moving, always needing some sort of stimulus. I cherished these comparisons as I always felt that I was different from my siblings. It was reassuring to know that there were other members in my family who 'got' me.

Garrett was later diagnosed with ADHD. The unfortunate part about Garrett's diagnosis is it instantly gave him an identity that overshadowed his authentic self. This ADHD became an element of who he was at home and at school. At the time, I was still young and did not fully comprehend what this actually meant and the consequences of such diagnoses. However, now as a teacher, I see so many people exclaim frustration when having to "deal with" ADHD as opposed to looking at how to embrace what makes ADHD individuals unique and truly understand how they learn and blossom best.

It is around this time of being diagnosed that a shift began to occur. Garrett was no longer Garrett.

You can put your mind into a hamster's wheel trying to figure what you could have done, what you didn't see, what someone did or didn't do, but at the end of the day that person is still not going to be brought back to life.

I remember the day like it was yesterday. I was in the middle of writing report cards. It was late, around 7:30pm and I was still at school. My cell phone had died but I was so immersed in my work, I didn't think about charging it. I received an email from my mom asking me to contact her as soon as I could. I went to the phone in my classroom and called her, not knowing what to expect. When I heard the words, "Garrett has died," I instantly felt pain. I have had family members die before. All four of my grandparents had already passed away, I had another cousin die tragically in a car accident when I was younger, but this was different. This was Garrett.

The rest of the week went by in a blur. I finished the report cards, worked the next two days and flew to Phoenix to attend the funeral.

No matter how old you are, it is always difficult to process and make meaning of an unnecessary death. What one can begin to do is instill purpose in their own life, find opportunities to share stories with others and develop a lens in which to view the world in a more hopeful way.

I have chosen to reflect on this heartbreak in the context of my career.

As a teacher, you tend to put a tremendous amount of pressure on yourself to identify those students who you think may be struggling. When you strip away all the other influences and reasons a person may choose to end their life, what it comes down to is that person is lost. I truly believe that identifying someone's passion and igniting that person's ability to identify a purpose in life is one of the most vital parts of being an educator. Since Garrett's suicide, I believe this even more so and continue to find ways to incorporate that message into my teaching and into my daily life.

This discovery will continue to drive my presence in the classroom and perhaps bring more meaning to Garrett's suicide. I have a desire to conduct research into the correlation between teen depression and suicide and the lack of fulfillment in one's life. More importantly, however, is to discover a way in which we can ensure youth will not experience that sense of hopelessness.

I may not ever be able to see one of the few people who 'got' me again, but he will forever be my guide.

Rachelle Savoie

Garrett,

My kindred spirit. My rambunctious twin. My beloved cousin. Even though we are eight years apart, growing up our families often commented on our similarities. Our energy and our outgoing personalities often got us into trouble, but also bound us together. By the time you were fully immersed in the stage of rebelliousness, I was a teenager and had let shyness prevail. Yet, I always felt my inner rebel come out when our families were visiting each other. I loved your spirit, your willingness to try anything and your loving nature. Although on the surface our relationship reflected one of a typical distant cousin relationship, I always felt a special connection to you. I know you did too as our time was often spent together tormenting my brother and your sister, even though they were closer in age to you.

When I came to visit your family in Arizona the spring of 2010 and your mom had told me you had isolated yourself from the people that love you the most, I felt that if anyone could reach you, it would be me. A phone call, a text, a few more texts. Each one was ignored. I didn't take it personally, I knew you struggled with asking for help, but I also knew you were like me--able to find the light in any dark moments. Your dark moment seemed to be lasting a bit longer than any I had experienced, but I was confident we shared this quality. I could have shown up on your doorstop, forced you to talk to me, your mom offered to give me your address. I opted to let you be, trusting I would see you later that summer during our annual visit. I have few regrets in my life. That I did not take every possible measure to see you that visit is one that will stay with me forever.

I will never forget the moment I received the phone call from my mom. I was writing report cards. It was about 7:30 at night and my mom knew I was working late, but the phone call could not wait any longer.

"Garrett committed suicide today."

The words echoed in my brain, not wanting to believe, begging them to disappear, to hear it was all a misunderstanding.

There was no misunderstanding. You were gone. Unable to grasp the light that was so near. You were doing better. I went to a psychic with your mom. I asked her if you were going to be okay. She lied! She had given me hope. I assumed we would have more time together and now you were gone. What kind of cousin was I? We were supposed to be kindred spirits. Instead, I felt like I had let you down.

I know I probably didn't surface much in your thoughts during this time. You were dealing with things I could never relate to and emotions you never felt comfortable to share with the people in your life. Know that you will not be remembered by this time. You will be remembered for being the carefree, hockey-loving, energetic and selfless person you were and will continue to be.

There has never been, nor will there ever be, a day I won't think about you. These moments often come at surprising times. Someone will say something, I will see a paintball reference, a Coyotes logo. These are the toughest moments because I don't expect them. But I also seek them out, wanting to hold your memory close by. I love you. I know I didn't say this enough when you were alive, but I say it now and will continue to say it as you will always hold a special place in my heart.

Rachelle Savoie

I stared at a blank screen for a while and just started writing this. I'm sorry if it seems off-the-cuff. Please use of it what you will. He's missed.

Garrett: I was working a late night at work when a phone call from my brother, Gavin, on the other side of the world came through with the news of Garrett's death. It knocked away all my stress and tiredness and B.S. and just hit me right in the gut. It just floored me.

I had to speak to other family members that night to get around to the idea of his death. It seemed so strange and unbelievable. I couldn't wrap my head around it.

I didn't know Garrett that well. I'd see him at large family reunions and always thought of him as a big, sweet, quiet kid. I still do. I always will. I wish I had spoken to him more. I wish I could have told him how his passing would have stunned the lives of people all over the globe, that it mattered to all of us, that he was an essential part of a greater fabric. His death was so unexpected and unnecessary. I wish I could have told him to give life more of a chance of it. Maybe it would have helped.

The few days leading up to the funeral were a daze as I thought of the circumstances of his passing and the pain his family were in. I hoped his soul was at peace and still do and think it is.

My wife and I watched his funeral online as it happened and wept helplessly throughout it. We thought Laurie, Tom and the kids were so strong throughout the service. They were so brave when faced with this tremendous loss.

Since the funeral, I've thought fondly of Garrett and the too-brief time I had with him, what I remembered to be a kind, gawky and handsome young man who didn't have a mean bone in his body. I would have liked to show him a bit of Europe if given the opportunity.

We know Garrett's good deeds and great heart will live on in the memories that his loved ones have of him and I know that the love and goodness in his life can be now channeled positively into a lesson to help others in similar situations.

When I think of the loss of Garrett, I'm always reminded of the testimony of three survivors of attempted suicides who had all realized immediately afterwards how easily solvable their problems were once they had leaped into the unknown. I wish more people in

Garrett's shoes knew this testimony and how much the life of one person means to hundreds of others, even if they don't believe it in those dark moments we all have.

Those are my thoughts on that lovely boy.

Blair Stewart

Dear Laurie, Tom, Kailee and Chantal,

When I received your request this past summer to write about your son and brother, Garrett, I did not have the emotional capacity or physical energy to answer your request.

Now, as the third anniversary of Garrett's death is close at hand, I am sending you some memories and thoughts that I have written down over the past few months, to show you that I care and love you all very much.

Gabrielle Racine Savoie

In Memory of Garrett Martin Savoie

August 30, 1991 – November 17, 2010

I am Gabrielle Racine Savoie, Garrett's great aunt, the wife of Dieudonne' Savoie, 1928 – 2013, the brother of Denis Francois Savoie, 1926 – 1993, Garrett's grandfather.

Our family lived in eastern Canada, Montreal, Sainte-Adele and Ottawa, many kilometers away from our western relatives in Vancouver, Edmonton, Calgary, California and Arizona. Although we did not get to meet all our relatives regularly, as family, we kept in touch by mail, telephone, internet, occasional trips, family reunions, weddings, deaths.

Our first meeting with Garrett was in 1995, a memorable event, a family reunion in Sainte-Adele, Quebec. The event, in the Laurentian foothills, brought the families of the three Savoie brothers from New Brunswick, Quebec, Manitoba, Alberta, and British Columbia. Garrett was 3 ½ years old. For three days, we ate meals together, we played games, we swam, and we shared memories and got caught up on everyone's lives and objectives and enjoyed the fresh air of Quebec.

Time moved on, and Don and I had the privilege to meet Garrett and his family in Canmore, Alberta at the wedding of his cousin Eric Metzler and Keri in 2001. A happy 10 year old enjoyed meeting aunts and uncles, grandmother Bernice, cousins and friends in the foothills of the Rockies. We also had the pleasure of meeting Garrett and his family at the beach in Florida. Tom, Laurie, Kailee, Garrett, Rachelle and Chantal had taken a Disney Cruise and we were wintering in Daytona. Tom and Don had planned a time and place to meet for lunch on the beach where the ship was in port. What pleasant memories I have of that short visit, and the children, eating hot dogs and fries, playing and running in the sand, another happy event.

A memorable occasion was undoubtedly another family reunion held in Ottawa – Gatineare in 2006. Three boys of a third generation born in 1991-1992, seven months of each other, Garrett from Arizona, Sean from Edmonton and my grandson, Justin from Quebec City, connected in an amazing manner. At that reunion, they developed camaraderie, an affinity that made me more aware than ever that family genes and bonds make for similarities in values and interests. The boys continued to keep in touch through the web and Facebook after the reunion from their three worlds, thousands of miles apart.

Where were we when we heard the news of Garrett's suicide? At home in Ottawa, we were getting ready for a trip to Australia (Sydney) to attend our youngest son Gregoire's wedding on December 11, 2010. Our doctor had just informed us that it would be unwise for Don to travel so far at this time, because of Don's medical condition. Though disappointed, I had arranged to travel to Australia with my sister Suzanne and Don encouraged me to go.

My reactions to the news was immense sadness, shock, anger, fear, concern about the effects such a tragedy has on all the members of the family. I did not ask the question "why" because I know only "One Person" can answer that critical question but we grieved for the family and for a lost young life.

I would like to be able to turn my world from hate to love, from greed to sharing, from despair to hope, from criticism to finding the good in each person from discrimination to acceptance of all our fellow men and women.

I would like to see bullying, intimidation and all the words that kill, banished from my world.

Every day, all over the world crimes against the person, the individual are prevalent. Incidents of violence have reached endemic proportions.

Intimidation starts in the back yards, in the schools, in sports, continues in society and the work place. This micro violence repeated daily often goes unseen, unobserved but can cause fear and deep anguish. It continues to be spread through television and the social media.

Our society's values have been eroded and the young people today have few role models. Nations are fighting nations for land and power, religions are fighting each other for supremacy, politicians are more interested in their own power than in their population's welfare and well-being, and business executives are more interested in profits than in their employees or customers.

In their formative years, young people need someone to look up to, to emulate, and to lead the path. Young people need to be listened to, they need acceptance for who and what they are. Young people need family, friends and faith, to be encouraged in their endeavors and dreams, given hope and love. They are entitled to their opinions, supported in their decisions and "Love".

In ending, I will tell you about our own experience of loss of a child.

Andre' was six years old when he was hit by a car near our home. The diagnosis was a contusion on the base of the brain stem. He lived for ten days on a breathing machine and died on my birthday, December 23. The neurologist told us to give all our love and attention to our four other children and to raise them well. Don and I did our best to follow his advice.

We were fortunate to have another child in 1969, Gregoire, and forty- six years later in 2012, Jessica, Gregoire's wife, gave birth to a boy whom they called Andre' Sean in Sydney, Australia.

Never a birthday passes without fond memories of our son, and I often ask him for help in coping with daily challenges.

You never forget, you grow, you become a better person, you appreciate what you have and you thank God for all his blessings.

May God give you courage and may you spread love in your family and all those around you.

Aunt Gaby

Chantal's Story

As I opened my notebook to begin writing, I realized that I am actually beginning something much greater than a note. I am writing about my healing process and reflecting it to you in a positive way.

It is one thing to be a friend or an acquaintance of someone who has committed suicide but let me tell you it is a totally different experience when you are actually part of the family. For me, I lost a brother on Wednesday November 17th.

So how does it feel to be the younger sister who has to continue to grow through the years that brought my brother so much pain and hurt? Let me tell you.

It was a Wednesday I will never forget. I, Chantal Savoie, had been at elementary school all day and I could hardly wait to get home. School for me was hell, and though I was never bullied or harassed I just couldn't stand it. This was a trait I shared with my late brother Garrett and to this day I still dislike it.

I remember running out of the gates of my elementary school into the front area where I always met my Dad. As a sixth grader all I was concerned about was what I was going to play when I got home. Little did I know that playing was going to be the least of my worries on this day.

I greeted my Dad with a smile. All my Dad said was, "Hello I have something to tell you." When I asked him what it was, all he said was, "I'll tell you when we get home." As any sixth grader would, I pestered him about it, asking if it was good or bad, would I be happy or sad? After three tries my Dad finally said, "It might make a few people sad." (His exact words.) I had no idea what it could be.

We pulled into the driveway. My Dad got out of the car and walked to my side and opened the door. I grinned a little as I was excited to hear the news, but thinking better of it, I wiped the smile off my face just in case it was bad news.

And bad news it was.

My Dad opened his mouth to speak. "Your brother is in heaven."

All the events of this horrible day are etched in my memory. I can tell you everything about it, my Dad had sunglasses on; I could tell you the color of his shirt, the color of my Mom's blouse, my amazing memory now felt like a curse! If you asked me to recall all the events of the day I could – from getting up in the morning to going to bed that night. I found myself wishing I were a bit more like my Mom and my sister who said to me they don't remember hardly anything about the day because they were shocked "off the planet". I remember thinking how lucky they were to not remember anything, but some silly small details of that awful day.

I remember standing in the driveway just after Dad had told me the news. The garage door started going up and I saw my Mom. I expected her to be the rock. She wasn't. I had never seen her so emotional before. I had never seen her cry that hysterically before. It was a cry that I learned to dread.

The days and weeks went by. We all got lots of support from our friends, both the kids and the adults. That really helped. I began to notice the difference between all of us – my Dad, my Mom, and my sister. My Mom and sister were very open and emotional and expressed all their feelings. My Dad and I were way more closed and didn't express ourselves like Mom and Kailee.

Personally, I did my best to forget about it. I could not and did not embrace it. This difference between my style of healing and my Mom's way really tore us apart. The little bit of relationship we had was shattered. Mom always wanted to talk to me about it, yet that was the last thing I wanted to do. Mom just could not understand it. We disagreed about it and fought about it all the time. I remember once thinking that I would never have an open relationship with my parents again.

To be honest, I still don't have a great relationship with them, but I am damn proud of where we have gotten!

I talked with my best friend and her parents, begging for advice on how to have a better relationship with my folks. It was the hardest time of my life. I didn't know how to talk with my parents. Everything I said or asked seemed to remind them of Garrett's death. Even asking if a friend could come over seemed to upset them. It seemed like this fear to talk to my parents came right from my brother's passing and now somehow I was stuck with making it better.

See how much can be affected by a stupid decision!

A lot of shit came along with loss of my brother and yet along with it came the best thing that has ever happened to me.

I was a twelve-year old kid dealing with the loss of my 19 year-old brother when an angel entered my life. That angel's name was Jessica LeAnn Thompson. Jessica taught horseback riding and rode at the same barn as me, the same barn where my horse Catti was boarded. One night Jessica and a bunch of other people came over to our house to help us cope. She and I went out back to the sports court behind my house. We scootered around and all the while I was oblivious to how much like me Jessica was. When she was fourteen her brother Scott died in a car accident. She had lost a sibling just like me!

In finding Jessica it was almost like I had found another sibling. To this day, I don't know where I would have been without her. I can honestly say for a while my relationship with Jessica was closer than my own blood sister.

You see Kailee had not been on the home scene very much. I was born when she was nine. When I was six she was fifteen and went off to boarding school for a year and then shortly after she went off to Kelowna for college and has just this year returned home. It was during this time that I needed her the most, 'cause all of a sudden I went from living in a family of five to being a single child. All of this change really took a toll on me.

I had to mature really fast because of this loss. Anyone who knows me would say how mature I am for my age. And even though Jessica was six years older than me we became best of friends. I even connected with Elle, Jessica's close friend who was seven years older than me!

Though some people would say the age difference wasn't healthy for me, I say it was. The truth is they helped me grow and mature as a person. They helped me heal and to be honest I think it is these two relationships that got me through this really tough journey. You see Jessica and Elle taught me how to overcome adversity. I saw their strength in overcoming their hard times and challenges. I saw how strong they were and this encouraged me to be strong too.

Although it was my plan and strategy to forget about this whole thing it wasn't God's plan. It seemed as if God wanted to work through it and to let it play out. And it did. When someone is gone like my brother Garrett, it felt like everything reminded me about him and usually at the most unexpected times. I had added the song "If I Die Young" to the music playlist at the funeral. That song really helped me at the time of the loss and at the funeral, yet after that I could not stand it.

It liked to kind of follow me around and I would hear it at the worst times and almost always in public places like the grocery store or in a friend's car. It is not just the song that gets to me though there are many things that remind me of my beloved brother:

Walking down the hall of my house and seeing the mark on the wall where I had measured our dog Daisy just four days before he died.

Seeing a license plate with his initials on it.

Even worse, going to the high school where he went, the same damn school that did this to my brother. Though I have made tons of new friends here, not a lot of them know this piece of my past. It is not an easy topic to just bring up in conversation.

Walking the same halls my brother did, seeing the same teachers that taught him, teachers I thought should have been able to stop him from committing suicide.

It is all so hard.

And yet even though it is tough I am strong and I am healing and getting stronger all the time. Yes I may have harsh opinions, but who wouldn't after something like this!

Now, a few years later I am noticing that high school can be great or it can be absolutely awful – it is up to me now to choose where I want to go with it all. I can either choose to make good decisions or bad decisions. But these decisions amount to more than just my reputation. How do you think it would look for my parents if two of their kids did drugs?

My parents aren't bad parents, in fact they are the best and I am blessed to have them. I feel like it is my job to step in and step up and keep my plate clean, which to be honest came as a result of my brother's bad choice.

So here I am in high school just like you perhaps, struggling with what choices to make. Some may be the same as yours some may be different, but we each have choices to make. Even though I have been through hell and back I am still faced with good choices or bad ones--just like you.

Learn from my brother's mistake just like I have. Pick the right path! Nothing can possibly be bad enough for you to make the same mistake Garrett did - a decision that has me writing this story to you.

Since his death my relationship with God has broadened. God is the greatest thing ever! God is always there for you especially when you think nobody else is. God listens and does not interrupt or argue. God does act on your prayers and helps in many ways. I find myself instantly becoming calm when I start a prayer. Take it or leave it-- you have the best coun- selor or therapist that ever lived right at your fingertips.

This whole thing was awful and I was really upset and angry. This was a shit thing to have to go through. It almost tore my family apart. Any one of us could have done the same thing as my brother did. Instead we got help, we are healing and we are once again opening up.

What I am trying to get at is suicide is really fricken' terrible and devastat- ing. If it has happened to your family or someone you love you CAN get through it just like I did. If you are thinking of taking your own life, don't! It is not worth it.

You are a beautiful person blessed with the opportunity to live in this wonderful world. Everything happens for a reason, so don't be so hard on yourself. It has been three years since I lost my brother and yes I am strong and a lot of good has come out of his death, yet if I could do any- thing to have him back here with me as I go through high school I would do it in a heartbeat.

Chantal and Garrett

Kailee's Story

It has been three years and I am still at a loss for words. Three years and I have no idea how to say everything that I want to and everything that I don't. Three years and I still refuse to accept that this is my life. I didn't ask for this.

On November 17, 2010 I received a phone call that changed my life. I was at the gym finishing a workout before I had to go to class. I knew that earlier that morning my brother, Garrett, had a court date to find out whether or not he was facing jail time for some drug charges that he had accrued earlier that year. I wasn't too worried because I was under the impression that the lawyer we had hired had assured us that if my brother stayed clean and sober it was unlikely that the judge would be very harsh on him. So when my Dad called, I assumed it would be to fill me in and tell me that everything was alright. The seriousness in his voice caught me off guard.

As I was leaving the locker room and heading out to the lobby, he asked if I was alone and able to talk. I told him that I would be in a second. I could tell that things had not gone the way we had planned and, thinking that Garrett was back in jail, I said, "I bet I know what you are going to say". My dad said, "No, I think you don't". As soon as I walked out the door, I asked what it was that he had to tell me.

"Garrett is dead". It's funny that I can remember the conversation before so perfectly, but the words that destroyed my world I can't recall that clearly. I do remember falling to the ground, screaming and pleading that this wasn't real and *no, please God*, this is not happening. In the midst of my screams and tears, my dad managed to tell me that he had shot himself. I asked who had found him and he told me my mom had. He also informed me that my Aunty Barbie and Uncle Glenn would be coming to get me (in Canada) and bring me home to Arizona and asked if there was anyone who could drive me to my house. I was so lucky that a friend of mine, Alexa, a true angel, had been at the gym and had heard me crying drove me to her house to grab Jen, another incredible friend, to drive me and my car to my house where Jordan was waiting for me. Head dripping wet and no shoes, she had answered my phone call while she was in the shower and met me at my house to help me pack, tell my professors I would be leaving, and then waited with me until my aunt and uncle arrived to take me home. On November 17, 2010, it was one bullet shot, but 5 lives had ended.

There are no words, no way to describe the deep pain that has consumed me from my brother's death. It is a suffocating, heart wrenching, crippling pain that I tried, but could not escape from. Death is supposed to be the final stage in life, a stop to suffering. But death had just become the introduction to mine.

While still in a state of shock, I made my journey home and prepared myself to plan my brother's funeral. Growing up, my mom had always said that if anything had ever happened to us that that would be it and she would be lying on the floor because life would no longer exist for her. My poor parents; while my own grief was insurmountable, my heart was breaking for them. And it was breaking for my sister, Chantal. My poor sister who had no idea of the turmoil our family had been going through for the past year (plus) with our brother and drugs and jail and now she had to find out that he was gone forever. She was only 12. I thought that I had to be the strong one, that I would take charge and make the hard decisions so that my family didn't have to.

When my aunt, uncle, and I arrived at my house the next day, I was so surprised to find about 50 people there. People taking turns to cook, clean, garden, contact friends and family, people helping to arrange the service and to just be there so we would not be alone. I had thought that I would be the strong one, but friends and family were there to be strong for us. I will truly never be able to express my gratitude and love for the kindness so many gave to us that week, and continue to give us to this day. It is sad though, that my brother didn't see the amount of people who loved and cared for him and who would be affected by his death. People who didn't even know him were affected. I knew at this time that his suicide would not be for nothing. That it would, in some way, someday, hopefully help other people. This could not have happened to us for no reason, but would become a sacrifice in order for others to avoid this tragedy.

I wish that I could say that this thought had inspired me to trudge forward in my life and start working to help make this into something positive. It didn't. My grief became accompanied by anger and guilt, which turned into more suffering. All I wanted to do was sleep, but I was afraid to because then I would be alone with my thoughts and more suffering.

I am sad because he is gone. My brother, who was wild and rambunctious, funny and kindhearted, easy going and sometimes a misfit, was gone. We were 16 months apart and for as long as I could remember he was always in my life, and I thought that he would always be. My brother who confided in me and let me visit when he pushed everyone else away had left me. About two weeks before he died, he had told me he was addicted to Percocet and that it was ruining his life. He had pushed everyone away and he was miserable. Times before we had talked and he had seemed so sure that no one understood him and anything that I said just made him angry. I remember him telling me the very words I had said and thought when I was 15 years old and in a similar place as him. It just never went through to him that I had been there and that feeling that way does not last and that we loved him and things could be better. But on this particular night, he understood. He told me he was quitting the painkillers cold turkey, and he did. For two weeks, it seemed that I had my old brother back. He called me every day as he struggled through the withdrawals, but was smiling because of how good he felt. That was the kind of person my brother was: strong, powerful, and joyful.

But something changed and I will never know for sure why. He took off, refused to speak to us again and I lashed out. I told him, when he didn't answer my phone calls and texts, that I knew he had relapsed and I was pissed. He called me one evening and this time I didn't answer. I didn't answer when he reached out to me one last time and now he is gone.

It haunts me to think about how sad, and scared, and alone he must have felt to think that dying was his best option. It tears me apart to think that I was not good enough to want to stay around for. It's selfish and irrational, but that is how I feel. I love him so much, and for a second I made him think that my love was conditional by not answering his call and I wasn't good enough.

And so I am angry. Fucking Furious. Do you know what it is like to try and pick up the pieces of your life after this? No note? No answer as to why when we gave him so many options for help? I don't want this burden. He may lay at peace, but what about us? What about those who are left behind? It never occurred to him to think that our mom would be the one to find his body. Did you really not care that she had to be the one to find you with half of your face gone? Does it not bother him that she will have that image with her forever? That I think about that too and try as I may I cannot forget?

And I know where he got the gun. At first, I felt bad that his best friends had just lost theirs, I felt truly sorry. But honestly, I have been so angry. I know they may have told me a story to make me, or possibly themselves, feel better about it. I wanted to believe it, but I am angry that they left him alone with a gun. I know it was his choice and again, it is selfish and irrational, but it's how I feel.

It's been hard waking up in the morning trying to care about things. I have found myself thinking that in no way, shape, or form, do I care or want to live anymore, but I am forced to because I have seen the aftermath, and I could never do this to my family again. I am angry that he took away that option for me, even if it's one I know I don't truly want to make. Because after he left, we found out he wouldn't have gone to jail, he would have had a year of unsupervised probation. So I have seen that as bad as things may get, as shitty as they seem, that they will always get better. This reminds me of how angry and screwed up the correctional system of the United States is, but that could be another book entirely.

I am sad watching our family try to redefine who we are after he has left. Watching my mom and dad take care of us through their own grief leaves me in awe. They are two of the most selfless, wonderful people I know. Any guilt they have over my brother's death they do not deserve because I have never seen two people so eloquently walk the line of having to show my brother that they would go to the ends of the world for him, but that he had to help himself as well. But they can't see that sometimes, because we are all still wondering what we could have done differently to avoid this.

Three years later and these words are still inadequate. Although excruciating, I must also express that this does not paint the whole picture. My brother's death has not let healing happen in a linear fashion. But healing has been happening. Not only has my family been an incredible pillar of strength, especially my sister, but there are some pretty important people whom, if it had not been for them, I wouldn't be able to write this today.

To Mitch, Stefan, and Jun: for picking me up at 2:30 am from the airport with Arby's in hand and adopting me into Narkscapes to take care of me when you hardly knew me.

To Jordan: for running out with no shoes and putting up with my selfishness and for being a true friend.

To Spencer, Chandler, and Alexa: for being there for me when I wasn't always easy to be around.

To Val, Kelsey, Libby, Jaki, Elyse, and Gill: I could seriously not imagine where I would be without you. You girls are my rock.

To Luke (and Elyse again): For the many therapeutic porch sessions, I owe you a kajillion dollars in therapy fees.

To Cheri and Abbey: You are an extended part of my family and I will always love you guys.

There is an enormous list of people whom I could thank and have probably forgotten to, but these are just a few of whom took care of me when I couldn't take care of myself. It took a tragedy to bring me to and, at times, pull me apart from these incredible people, but without my brother leaving I may have never been able to appreciate or know what it means to be a true friend.

If I can stress one thing that I am working through now, it is forgiveness. Three years ago, forgiveness was enough. Forgiveness may have changed the outcome for my family and forgiveness may have prevented me from choosing to deal with my pain the way I have after my brother died. But I am learning to forgive myself and my brother and I am seeing how that forgiveness is opening all kinds of possibilities for love instead of hurt. It isn't always easy, but forgiveness can always be a beginning for anyone.

I love you G Man and I miss you so much. I will see you again.

Love always,

Kailee Savoie

Kailee and Garrett

November 21, 2010 – The speech Kailee gave at Garrett's Memorial:

For as long as I remember, I have been blessed to have my brother by my side – my partner in crime. As his big sister, I have been told that it was I who he looked up to and it was up to me to be there and help guide him through life. The truth is, it was he who taught me so much and I could not be who I am without him.

My brother was the most passionate person I have known in life. He had the most contagious, almost rambunctious energy that could not be contained. From bouncing off the walls and chasing me around the house when we were younger to exploring historical ruins and annihilating people with paintballs, he was always ready to embrace the moment and go all out. It's funny, though, how he could slow down and channel all of that energy into learning something new about the world like baking with my mom at 3 years old or playing a game of crib with my dad.

In every relationship he had, Garrett was a kind, caring and loyal friend, brother, son, cousin and nephew. He may not have outwardly expressed these things, but just by sitting next to him these qualities would emanate from his core. The most obvious way he showed his love was by making people laugh. You could always count on him for those random one-liners that could make you smile and happy no matter what the circumstances were at the time.

The thing I admire the most about him is that he was true to himself, and the other Garrett I saw was the same Garrett as when he was 2. He did not care what anyone thought and he did what was true to his heart. I am still in awe of the honesty and courage it takes to do this, yet I don't think he even realized that it is so rare to find someone who is so real like that in this world.

As painful as all of this is now and as unfair as this all seems, I know Garrett would want only happy and better things to come out of this for everyone. As lonely and hard as life may seem, tomorrow is always a new day and if you look around, life is full of people who love you and are impacted by you.

G-MAN, I love you so much and miss you like crazy. I hope you see now how powerful you are and I know you will be with me for the rest of my life. We all love you and you owe me a hug BIG time. Rest easy and in peace. I love you.

Frozen moments: My recollection of those 24 hours.

The call.

My scream brought my wife running into our office. I remember three total strangers turning to look at me, totally exposed emotionally. Barb is already in tears just hearing the anguish in my voice. Unaware of the horrible words yet unspoken. My wife's' beautiful face folds in on itself and simultaneously her legs begin to collapse.

Hurry, we have to get to Kailee and get her home.

The airport. I see them first. From a hundred feet away they are just a tall man waiting with his little daughter for family to arrive. Closer now, it's Tom. I don't want to look at him. I am afraid to see his pain, mine is enough. Yes, I see the pain, but god damn, I see the will in him to be strong. Just like him, quiet but strong. Then I think of the call he had to make to me, the strength that took.

Hurry we have to get to Laurie.

The kitchen.

Dread, yet I am in such a rush. I should have been here sooner for my sister. I should have spent more time here. I am a terrible brother. Hurry. So many people. I can hear them all talking. It's like a party. Oh my God, he didn't just have to call me! How many of these people did they have to call? How many times did they have to say it? Where is she? In the kitchen. I can't hold her close enough. Her sweater is warm and damp. Great heaving sobs like I have never cried in my life. More than I cried for my mother, my father, my beloved grandmother. Why? Because it is so unnatural. They are going to have to bury their son. Who fucking does that? And how?

Glenn

Section 3: **FRIENDS**

Friendship—it's something as people we all seek out. Friendship is what we depend on to help create our character and mold us into the people that we will eventually become. Sometimes friendships are long-lasting and others are brief encounters, but either way friendship is a very important part of living life and building character. The entries in this section are from Garrett's friends. They each have their own interpretation of the special relationship that they had with him, but one thing is clear as each friend poignantly discusses how one young man's life and death has impacted their own—he will be missed and the memories that he created with these people will never die. They are like all friendships in the world—they are created by a bond and live on through memories. What these entries discuss is the love and good times experienced throughout the friendship and also the dark shadow that has crept into their lives since the premature departure of a dear friend.

Alright. Garrett was my best friend; I'll never forget the endless nights we spent playing Halo and me getting pissed because he always beat me. I'll never forget how he was a real person, always up front and honest, except when he started doing the pills, etc. It changed him as a person and it was hard to watch. I also feel this is partly my fault for not being more assertive. He called me a week before he took his life and asked me if I wanted to hang out and I said no because I told him before if he kept doing what he was doing, I no longer wanted to be a part of his life. I had a dream a couple weeks ago, it was incredibly vivid. In my dream, I was at a hotel with all my friends, drinking and celebrating. In the midst of all that I turn around and there's Garrett looking right at me with a sort of apologetic smile on his face. He seemed to appear out of nowhere. I was speechless and in my dream, the tears started flowing uncontrollably. We went outside and I dropped to my knees and began crying in front of him. I asked with pleading eyes and trembling voice, "Garrett, where have you been man, where have you been?" He pulled me up and hugged me. He said, "I am *so* sorry, I didn't mean to leave you." I began sobbing uncontrollably, "I know man, I know," he said. I don't remember much after that and I woke up with tears in my eyes. That was the most powerful dream I think I've ever had. He taught me how to be myself and think more logically about things. Like I said, I will never forget him...

Bill

I remember, and will never forget, my first funeral of a friend who took her life. We were in our sophomore year of high school and, like all teenagers, life at times would feel unfair or even hopeless with all these new changes and expectations people had of us. At that age, none of us really knew the repercussions of suicide and the effects it would have on family and friends. Her funeral is my first sad memory and it changed my outlook on suicide forever. After seeing her family in such grief, I knew I could never make that decision for myself. Through the years, more and more children from the Cave Creek community school district (especially Cactus Shadows High School) have committed suicide. I had known several of those that sadly lost their lives to depression or drug use and, though their stories were different, the aftermath following their passing were all the same--with words left unsaid; memories that were never made; and futures that were never taken advantage of. Carrying such sadness is hard to do every day, especially if it's carried along and unfortunately passed down to the families and friends. We will help carry it together. We will forever miss and love those that we've lost to suicide and honor their lives by living ours to the fullest. I just hope others read these entries and know if they are thinking of making that decision that they realize it deeply impacts those around them. I know some might not see the positives when they are at their lowest, but if only they would reach out to someone before, maybe they would be reminded that they are never alone.

Jessica Terpening

Garrett My Guardian Angel

You found me when I was in my darkest place
You took me under your wing with enormous grace
Now you have gone without a trace
And left my heart with an empty space

What about maple leaves you'll never get to touch
And Mr. Awesome who misses you so much
No more cutting branches off the trees
No more ketchup with Mac and cheese

Here I am learning how to cope
Alone with a feeling of lost hope
Looking for your shining light
To help me make it through each night

In my dreams you hold my hand
We walk on the beach with just our toes in the sand
You embrace me and hold me tight
And then I awake and you're nowhere in sight

Looking at your picture makes me cry
Thinking that no one should ever die
I wonder what God has in store for me
If an angel is what he needed you to be

Hilary

One Day

Every day the sun comes to shine
A start the game of seek and find
Every time I hear a sound

All I do is look around

I know you hear me when I call

I feel you when the maple leaves fall
You push me to help in any way I can
It will happen according to your plan

I will see your smiling face proud
When I finally come to meet you behind the white fluffy cloud

Hilary

Laurie,

Thank you so much for reaching out to me and everyone else with this amazing idea in memory of Garrett. I was touched reading your letter and I would love to be a part of the book. Here are a few things I would like to share...

I met Garrett in middle school and he was a peer of mine for many years. We had classes together and he was always a pleasure to be around. I was shy in high school, so I didn't get close to many people, but I always thought Garrett seemed so non-judgmental and kind. I would definitely say he was one of the nicest people I knew.

When I found out about his passing, I was truly shocked and upset. It is heartbreaking seeing all the pictures of him with his family, that big smile, and wishing he could have hung in and moved past whatever he was going through.

About a year after Garrett's death, I was having a rough night. I remember crying and praying to Garrett. I do not know if I just wanted to imagine it, or a miracle really happened, but I then felt him hug me and a faint image of him flash in front of me. Now when I think back to him, I just remember the warm feeling and comfort I received in my moment of grief. Even when he is gone he is still making a difference.

I feel I can relate to Garrett in some ways. I battled depression for about five years. I didn't express to anyone what I felt inside, and even though I wished I could get help at times, I was too weak emotionally to do so. I eventually woke up and realized how beautiful life is and what a gift it is to have. I am completely changed now, but in high school especially, I felt hopelessly trapped in my own body.

To anyone out there reading who may struggle with depression, I beg that you please don't do what I did and keep it to yourself. Do not think that taking your life is the way out. There are understanding people out there who want to help you find happiness. I look back now and realize the battles I went through made me stronger, more mature, and helped me to reach my dreams and realize the importance of life. Anything is possible. Keep dreaming and your life will change. Reach out to your loved ones, they want to be there for you. Don't be afraid to show you're hurt. There is a brighter tomorrow and I have found it, you can too. My heart goes out to Garrett's family and friends. May he always be remembered.

Love, Jessica Lehr - Designer of *The Ripple Effect*

I met Garrett in middle school at Sonoran Trails. I came over a few times and also knew Kailee. I first heard about his passing at home from a buddy. I was shocked to hear the saddening news. I've had two other buddies commit suicide and I was just wondering why?

I still am surprised to this day and still saddened every time the subject comes up.

It's changed my life in the aspect of trying to spend the most time with your friends you can because you don't truly know what is going on in their head. So enjoy the time you can with them because you never know what will happen. It always seems to be the ones too, that seem happy, but in a day things could change....

Tyler McClendon

I hope this helps. I miss the kid. Bless you guys and sorry for your loss =(

Hi Mrs. Savoie. My name is Corey. Garrett was a good friend of mine when we were in high school. I just recently heard about what happened :(so I guess it's better to be late than to never voice my condolences to you and your family. I am very sad and sorry for the loss of a great person.

-Corey P

I met Garrett in our junior year of high school at Cactus Shadows. We shared a couple of classes together. Garrett was always a good friend to me. I wasn't the greatest friend to him in return, though. I never thought that his drug habits would take the turn it did and I feel slightly responsible for his drug usage. I also never thought he would end up doing what he did. Garrett was always happy when he was around me even when he had the right to hate me. When I heard about Garrett's death, two and a half years had already passed. I was at a loss for words and very confused. I don't think anyone saw that coming. Well at least I didn't. I hadn't seen Garrett since the end of our first semester of our senior year. I really miss him, especially with the thought that I will never get to see him again. I will never get the chance to apologize to him for any of the ways I had wronged him as a supposed friend. Again Mrs. Savoie, I am incredibly sorry for your loss.

I grew up with Garrett. We were practically siblings and that is the way we treated each other. We picked on each other, played Mario Cart on the Play Station, did our homework together, and always had family dinners and gatherings. The Ortmans and the Savoies were one family. We both attended Cactus Shadows High School; however, we grew apart because of our busy schedules and social lives. We worked together at Jalapenos, but it was still just a "hello" and "goodbye." I knew we had different interests and different groups of friends at this time. When I heard about his death, I was shocked, but in the back of my head, I knew Garrett was struggling. When the Savoies came over for our usual family gatherings, he never came with them anymore. He was slowly drifting away. Although it was hard to accept, I will never forget about those wonderful childhood memories I shared with Garrett. He will always be my big brother at heart. Always.

Taylor Ortman

Laurie,

I love this book idea. Garrett is on my mind a lot & continues to be a part of my life. There is a great organization called notmyKid.org run by Steve & Debbie Moak, I think it would be great to see if there can be a partnership with them for this book. The month of Ramadan began this week, & in honor of Garrett I will be donating $500 in his name to the organization. Thank you for the letter candle, I am excited to be a part of this Project. :)

Card from Abraham

I first met Garrett in a middle school gym class. I was new to the city, moving from the west side of Phoenix and Garrett immediately opened up his friendship to me. That friendship lasted until November 17, 2010.

Garrett was my closest childhood friend. We often went to the theaters, played airsoft battles, and spent too many hours playing computer games. From the moment I first met Garrett he has taught me so many things I still hold dear to this day. His loyalty as a friend was unquestionably his greatest asset to me. No matter what mood I was in, Garrett's cheerful personality always lifted my spirits. My fondest memories of Garrett were when we were simply together at night looking up at the stars talking about the past, present and future. We both loved to look at the stars. We found it relaxing staring up at the darkness waiting to see a shooting star and just watching the stars flicker. It made us appreciate the vastness of our world. Garrett was a deep and thoughtful individual. His philosophy on life was something many people didn't get a chance to see. It came out when you were alone with him and engaged in deep conversation.

Our friendship began to fade during senior year of high school. As I was focusing on increasing my abysmal grades, Garrett was focused on other things. I often look back and feel as if I abandoned my best friend during his darkest hours to selfishly focus on myself.

Even though Garrett and I stopped hanging out and talking with one another, he was always on the back of my mind, and I always knew that if I were in need of help I could rely on him. Looking back, I wish I could have reciprocated.

The day Garrett passed away I received a phone call from a close friend of mine, she had also been friends with Garrett at one point. When she told me the news, I remember I had just finished for the day at ASU and began to head to my car when my phone rang. She told me the news and I remember standing silently. I was in disbelief. While on the phone with her I began to get upset, especially with Garrett. So many questions were running through my mind and I knew none of them would ever be answered. I sat in my car staring outside with tears running down my cheeks. It was finally beginning to sink in that my childhood friend was gone, and I was never going to see him again. There would no longer be any reminiscing of our lives together, any late night stargazing chats – there would only be memories.

When the day came for Garrett's funeral, I remember getting a phone call from my friend who informed me of his passing, asking me if I was going to attend. I cowardly refused. Perhaps it was the shock and pain of his death still affecting me, or my anger at him at the time still. I couldn't muster myself to go, even though his service was a few blocks from my house. Looking back, I wish I had gone. I wish my friend had pushed me to attend. However, nearly three years later, this is my way of saying goodbye to Garrett.

Dear Garrett,

I miss you. Your friendship and loyalty is one in which any friend dreams to have. I wish I could have been there and helped you. I'm sorry I wasn't. I miss our stargazing conversations, and I wish more people could have gotten to see the side of you that I knew all too well. Now that you are among the stars and in the heavens, I look forward to the day where we once again meet and look towards the vastness of space and converse about our lives and reminisce about our childhood. Your friendship has made me a better man and you will always be a part of my life, in this one and the next.

Sincerely,

A.J.H. Abraham Hamadeh

Dear Garrett,

Where do I begin? I feel like I have let you down in so many ways. I wish that I could have been a better friend to you and I wish that you would have come and talked to me. I would have done absolutely anything to help you and I know a lot of people feel the same way. November 17th will remain the worst day of my life. We were waiting for you to come over and hang out. Instead of getting a call from you, we got a call from your mom. I stopped breathing and time stopped moving. To say I was in shock would be an understatement. I didn't know what to do. I couldn't believe what I had just heard. All I kept thinking was that I saw you last night, how could this be true? It must be a mistake. I kept waiting for you to walk through the door. I am not sure how I made it through the week. I remember being in a trance. I didn't move. I just sat there. The only time I got up was to numb my pain. The first time I left the house was to attend your funeral. It was such a beautiful service. I cried the entire time. After that, I stayed in bed for weeks. I didn't want to be awake in a world that you weren't a part of. I dreamt of you every single time I closed my eyes. I wanted you back so bad that even with my eyes open I didn't see the world around me. All I saw was you. The regret I felt was too much to bear. All the fights we had played through my mind and all the hurtful things that had been said were on a replay that I constantly heard. I wanted to take it all back. I said the things I said because I loved you and I didn't like to see you head down the path you were on. I will never forget the last thing you said to me. You gave me a big hug and looked me in the eyes and told me that everything was going to be okay, that life would all turn out how it was supposed to and that I would be okay.

At the time, I didn't realize this was your goodbye or our reconciliation. I've kicked myself over and over for not realizing this that night. I've heard it countless times that it's natural to blame yourself, to think you could of stopped this and they tell me the same thing--nothing I could have done would have changed your mind. I still don't believe this. I just wish I could go back in time. I would sell my soul to save yours.

Every day I think of you. I can still close my eyes and hear your laughter, see your smile and feel your presence. I am so lucky I got to see you on a daily basis. I wouldn't trade anything for the memories that I have of us. You were the person I could spill my soul to. All I ever thought about was how cool it would be 50 years from now to still have you in my life. You consumed every thought of the future that I had. I never thought you wouldn't be here. You will always be a part of me and with me in everything I do. Your suicide changed my whole life. I appreciate everything I have way more than I ever did before. I want to live my life to the fullest, for myself and for you. You taught me the true meaning of love and how important it is to love with your whole heart. I would wish no one the pain I have felt and continue to feel. I think about you at all the times of the day and always wonder what you are doing in heaven. I know you have impacted so many people's lives and have changed the future of others. God has a bigger and better plan for you than anyone could have imagined. As you know, death was something I could not fathom. Now, I no longer fear death but wait until the day that I can be taken to you.

Anonymous

Dear Garrett,

I remember having dinner with you one night at your parent's house. You were so relatable, laid back, and sweet to talk to. I loved hearing your infectious laugh and your responses to my dad's silly and never ending questions. I have memories of you from home videos and stories I have heard from family members. I heard you committed suicide when I was in Ohio in my sister Lindsay's room. I started to bawl, unable to comprehend what had happened. I wish I had gotten to spend more time with you, but from the time I did have with you, I know you were an amazing, kind and genuine person. I am grateful our families are such great friends. Your family and friends love you more than you could ever know. Each of the Savoies have a special place in my heart.

Love,

Abbie Stream

Garrett,

From what I have heard about you, we would have had a lot in common. I wish we could have hung out and played hockey and paintball together. I am excited to meet you in heaven.

Love,

Ben Stream

Hi Laurie,

I knew Garrett from school. Middle school through high school. Although we weren't close friends, I sat next to him for a big part of math junior year and got to know him a little better. He was always happy and made my least favorite subject easier to get through. I was extremely shocked when I heard what had happened. I still don't really believe it because Garrett always seemed so carefree and happy. It's hard to believe that he was so unhappy or had something so big going on that he would choose to take his own life. I check in on his Facebook page from time to time and I'm not 100% sure why. Part of me feels like all of the students from CSHS who have taken their lives may be back on there someday, like it was all a nightmare and didn't really happen. Part of me likes to see all of the amazing things people have to say about Garrett or David or anyone else. I love the idea behind this book because this is such a hard thing to understand and grasp. I hope that it can help your family heal and help others who will sadly have to go through the same thing. Thank you for reaching out to Garrett's community. He is definitely with you through this process.

Kelcey Peterson

Dear Garrett Savoie,

As Steve Jobs once said, "You can't connect the dots looking forward, you can only connect them looking backwards. So you have to trust that the dots will somehow connect with your future. You have to trust in something, your gut, destiny, life, whatever. Because believing that the dots will connect down the road will give you the confidence to follow your heart, even when it leads you off the well-warned path and that will make all the difference...

Remembering that you are going to die is the best way I know to avoid the trap of thinking you have something to lose... No one wants to die, even people who want to go to heaven don't want to die to get there, and yet, death is the destination we all share, no one has ever escaped it. And that is as it should be, because death is very likely the single best invention of life, it's life change agent, it clears out the old to make way for the new. Right now, the new is you. But someday, not too long from now, you will gradually become the old and be cleared away... Your time is limited; so don't waste it living someone else's life."

If I had the chance to see you once more in this lifetime, I'd hope to show you this letter and these quotes that I share and that they would give you peace of mind and explain what I think about life. I remember we met through high school, and if I remember correctly, we had more than a few classes together, Video Technology being the most memorable. We hung out numerous times outside school. Better to me than a just a classmate, you were a damn good friend. I was deeply saddened when I heard the news of your suicide. I specifically remember being at work the day I heard the tragic news. A fellow friend informed my manager, who then informed me of the devastating news and let me take the rest of the day off. I couldn't convince myself to go home, for my home was not exactly a home in itself at the time (family problems). Instead, I called a good friend of mine who knows me best and let him know what had happened. He then immediately invited me over.

To this day, my thoughts are still in disbelief. I could never have imagined this to happen to you. Your action has caused me to value life much more than I did at the time. I was personally caught up in the teenage socializing life: under aged drinking, drugs, and popularity. I was experimenting with what was around me. Even being caught up, I was dealing with some issues at my home. I forgot who I was and why I had sometimes considered doing harmful things to myself. However, knowing you personally and seeing what you left on this earth made me think twice about some of the decisions I was making. Your death allowed me to appreciate the things I have in this life because there are times where we all take life for granted. If it was not for the support of my friends, family, and music, I honestly do not know if I'd be alive to this day.

There are a few songs I wish to refer to, the first of which is by Flogging Molly (If I Ever Leave This World Alive).

"If I ever leave this world alive I'll take it for the things you did in my life. If I ever leave this world alive I'll come back down and sit beside your feet tonight. Wherever I am, you'll always be, more than just a memory, if I ever leave this world alive!... I'm okay; I'm all right, though you have gone from my life. You said that it would; now everything should, be all right."

The second is by Oasis (Wonderwall).

"Today is gonna be the day that they're gonna throw it back to you. By now you should have somehow realized what you got to do. I don't believe that anybody feels the way I do about you now... There are many things that I would like to say to you, but I don't know how. Because maybe, you're gonna' be the one that saves me." These lyrics make me take a second look from other points of view outside of my own.

I have been asked "What keeps you here on this earth, what keeps you alive?" In my response, it's the fact that I can face difficult decisions which I've had in my life with the knowledge that life still goes on. Even when days aren't going my way, I can still keep a smile on my face and hold my head high because I know that some things are just out of my control. My mind has been racing for over two and a half years about what had happened. I wish for the chance to go back in time and get to know you more. For now, I can only appreciate the times we had while you were alive. Over time, I have been saddened, but yet at peace; saddened because you are a good friend to me, yet at peace because I know you are an angel looking down from the heavens.

Your dearest friend,

Christian Zundel

A Better Place

By Mandi Gleason

    I remember the moment that I learned Garrett had passed away like it was yesterday. I was working as a barista at a local deli in Wilmington, North Carolina. It was a gloomy and cold day, so naturally the business was slow. On days like that, I passed the time on Facebook. However, that day my head was somewhere else. My thoughts were with one of my best friends, Nicole. The next day would mark two years since she had taken her life. I remember thinking how much my life had changed since my sophomore year in high school and I was smiling to myself at how surprised she would be at where I was in life. The things that we thought were so crucial--going to the best party on Friday night and hoping that this week's crush would notice us--were of such little importance now that I couldn't help but wonder why we cared so much. Suddenly, something on Facebook caught my attention. My friend Allie had posted "R.I.P. Garrett." My stomach did a somersault. Post after post from my friends in Arizona read the same. I frantically searched for Garrett's profile and my fears were confirmed: my beloved friend Garrett had passed away. Nothing on Facebook told me how he had died, but in the back of my mind I knew. It wasn't long until I confirmed that he had committed suicide. My mind was racing. Why did he take his life? What if I had never moved to North Carolina and had stayed in Arizona? Would he still be alive? I probably would have still hung out with him every day. What had gone wrong since I moved? I left only six short months ago. How could he do this to his family? How could he do this to his friends? How could he do this to me?

    As these thoughts consumed me, an elderly man came to the counter to buy a cup of coffee. I tried to compose myself, but didn't succeed. He asked me if there was something on my mind. Normally, I would have smiled and told him I was just tired from a long night of studying, but I knew there was no way I could pull off that white lie. So, I told him the news. The man told me that even though it was a shame Garrett had died, he was no longer in pain and in a better place. Even though I knew that the sweet old man was just trying to make me feel better, his words ignited a fiery rage inside me. I thought I was going to have a meltdown right there in the middle of the deli. What about all of his friends and family? In one instant he had put all of us in pain and in a horrible place! How could Garrett be so selfish? He had so many people that loved and cared about him and I felt like he had just slapped us all in the face.

Over the next few months, I began to learn what it meant to hate someone and yet still love them. Every time I thought about how angry I was with him and how selfish I thought he was, I felt so horrible for thinking those thoughts. I knew that he must have been hurting badly and that he must have thought that suicide was the only way he could end his pain. How could I be mad at someone who just wanted to stop hurting? When Nicole died, I didn't have those feelings of anger; I only felt sorrow and mourned her death. With Garrett, it was a completely different story. Sure, I was distraught and lamented his death, but my feelings of anger and rage dominated every other emotion.

I kept playing the last time I saw Garrett over and over in my head. He seemed so normal and so happy. Why wouldn't he confide in me? We were such good friends. He knew that he could come to me when something was bothering him, just as I came to him when I needed someone. Those thoughts always brought me back to the belief that things might have been different if I had stayed in Arizona.

As time passed, my rage began to morph into something else: blame. I began to feel more and more responsible for what happened to Garrett. I let those thoughts push me further and further into a deep, dark, and somber hole. Two of my best friends had committed suicide. I was a good friend to each of them. I was the common denominator so I must be to blame. This thought process continued for one grim year.

Thankfully, my feelings over the past year have evolved into something else entirely. Ironically enough, an ad for depression medication was the catalyst for my changed attitude. The girl in the ad was sitting in a dark room wearing a big, baggy sweatshirt. She was just sitting there, looking out the window. The girl reminded me of myself. Why was I letting this dominate my thoughts? I was letting the sadness and sorrow that had consumed Garrett continue when I should be letting the joy and happiness that once filled Garrett's eyes live on instead! I began thinking about Garrett's big smile that lit up his entire face. I thought about all of the fun memories of him that I had forgotten over the past year and a half. I grinned, thinking about his ridiculous laugh. I imagined Garrett smiling and laughing in heaven. I finally understood what the old man in the deli meant when he said, "He is no longer in pain and in a better place."

I am sorry that I didn't get in touch with you earlier. I don't use social media as much as I used to. I did mention I wanted to try and contribute something so I reached out to some old friends to try and see if we could. Although we all had a few good memories of times we would hang out, we couldn't think of anything that would do justice. To be honest, I would only have brief things to say because I lost touch with everyone when I moved to Tucson.

If you would like to include my last memory of hanging out with him you can, but I would understand if it wasn't what you were looking for.

I remember seeing him at a party the last few nights before I left town and we didn't recognize one another at first because it had been awhile since the last time I saw him. He didn't care that he wasn't sure if he knew me, he smiled and got talking about random stuff until we remembered hanging out before. I was glad, too because I didn't know many people there and it was helpful to feel like I belonged. I will always appreciate that.

I'm sorry that I didn't get back to you sooner. Much luck on the book project, I hope it comes out the way you had hoped.

Michael Pospisil

I met Garrett the summer before senior year of high school. I knew of him before, but then we met, and I really knew him. I thought, how could I have missed this human roaming around this campus and this town and not introduce myself? He was so....good. I remember the night we made it "official". The place was Dynamite Park and it was late on a Friday. We both had to be home soon so we broke away from the group. We sat face-to-face, cross-legged on top of a picnic table under a bright green Palo Verde tree. He nervously reached for my hands and I gave them to him.

"Be my girlfriend," he said. It wasn't a question. It wasn't a demand. It was him saying he needed this to happen. My stomach fluttered and I smiled, I smiled big.

"Okay" I said, still smiling. We sat there as long as we could, and then he took me home.

That memory of my first love blooming will stay with me and haunt me forever. We went through the motions, took our time getting to know each other and teaching each other how to be in a relationship. He met my mom, my brother fell in love with his company...finally another boy around the house. I met his parents. I didn't know then how much Laurie and Tom would come to mean to me in life, however distant. I met his sisters, Kailee who I'd known through mutual acquaintances, and Chantal, the adorable slightly annoying kid sister who bided my time when Garrett would allow it. Their relationship always made me laugh. He pretended he hated her company, but I always caught his secret smiles when she would say or do something silly. His secret smiles were so perfect.

Then he changed. He was never happy; never the relaxed and hilarious individual I'd fallen in love with. On Valentine's Day, our plans got ruined, but we ended up making the best of it--ordered a pizza at his parent's house and stayed all dressed up and ate with the lights dimmed down. It was fun. Garrett went to his room and when I went to find him, I saw him swallowing a few pills. I was furious. Of all people, he had to go get caught up in the madness of Oxycodone and Percocet. Then it all started to make sense. I screamed at him for being such a complete and utter idiotic bastard. He cried, apologized, asked for my support. I tried.

We tried to work through the addiction, but I couldn't help him. He gave me a letter saying how sorry he was and he wanted to stop. But he didn't really...the addiction was too strong. I cried for us. I cried for him. I made the decision to break up just before senior prom. I wasn't strong enough to help him. I was too young and so was he. So, I bailed. I did what was best for me and I left him alone in the black hole he had sucked himself into. I'm sorry for that every day of my life. Then come the "maybes." Maybe he would have gotten better if I stuck around and helped him through it. Maybe I could have been of some motivation to get better, seek help. Those "maybes" keep me up at night still, 5 years later.

I moved on with my life, we completely lost touch. He even deleted me off of Facebook so I was completely in the dark about his addiction. Little did I know, it had only gotten worse. More pills and then a rumor that he dabbled with heroin. I still don't know whether that is completely true, but when I think about him lolling his head after a big hit, I can't breathe, so I try not to picture it. I thought of him often, and of his family. Every now and then, my brother would ask, "Sis, where is Garrett?" and all I could think to say was "I dunno, buddy. I haven't seen him in a long time, I think he's lost." He was lost. He wasn't Garrett.

In my sophomore year of college, I was driving home pretty late one night with my boyfriend, Alex. He knows Garrett, knows our past. My phone rang and it was a number I didn't know. I answered. I remember the conversation perfectly.

"Hello?" I said.

"Hi, this is a friend of the Savoie family. Is this Allie?" The stranger said quietly. I remember thinking how strange it was to have him call so late at night. Maybe the Savoies were doing some event and needed volunteers. My brain was thinking of everything besides what was to come.

"I have some scary news for you. Are you seated?" I was seated, parked in my spot with Alex staring at me wondering what was happening.

"Yes. Okay." And then it hit me before the stranger said it.

"I'm so sorry, Laurie and Tom asked me to call you...Garrett has passed away. He committed suicide in his apartment." Utter shock. Immediate tears. I hadn't even seen him in two years, but my heart ripped into two pieces when I registered what had just been whispered into my ear.

"Okay." I had to let go and cry.

"If there is anything I can do for you, please don't hesitate to call. Again, I'm so sorry."

"Thank you. Tell them I'm sorry." I hung up. The tears were flowing freely, but quietly. Alex sat next to me still, more confused than ever. I told him the news and he came around to my side and practically carried me into the house. I called my mom who had always been fond of Garrett. We cried together. The next few days were full of spreading the news to mutual friends. It was painful to hear how loved Garrett was and that he was gone in spite of it.

Now that I've told my story, I'd like to write down what I'd say to Garrett if I had one chance to do so.

Garrett,

I wish I had known your pain. I wish I could have helped. Your death was traumatic for everyone who knew you, even just an acquaintance. But for me, I felt sorry for you. You could never accept the love that you were given. I felt sad for you that you were so insecure, so unsure of yourself and it made you wonder if you could trust someone to love you. Even your own parents, your sisters... you just couldn't believe that people could love you unconditionally despite your flaws. I was one of those people. I always was and I still am. I was angry for a while. If I really think about it then I get angry again. Sometimes I think about your funeral when Casey Curtis had to hold me up by my elbows because my sobs were taking all of my energy. When I watched your sisters put on their brave faces and remember your life so beautifully. When I had to hug your mother who couldn't see my face or hear my well wishes through her tear-blurred eyes. When I had to hold your father's hands and tell him how sorry I was and he could hardly look me in my eyes for fear of losing himself to his emotions. That's when I get angry. I think to myself, how could a boy who was so good, so sweet...do this to his family and his friends. I try to remember that you were lost and couldn't even tell me what you were thinking even if you wanted to. There is a lot of back and forth when I think about you, but I've come to accept that this happened. You left us in the worst way possible and all I can do now is think about the good memories and try to push the horrible ones away when they resurface. The one thought that I can't push away is how I'll never be able to talk about you to my future children. I won't get to tell my daughter about my first love and tell her how wonderful it is. I won't get to tell my son what a gentleman you were and how he should follow your example on how to treat a young woman. I don't get to talk about the first time I ever loved a boy because I don't know how to explain to a pre-teen that you killed yourself. I'm sorry for both of us for that. I love you and miss you Garrett and I would give a whole lot to say that to you and for you to be able to see the love that you gave up.

Allie

11/17/13

Dear Garrett,

I sit here to write you and am bewildered as what to say. Never, in my wildest of dreams, would I have imagined you disappearing from my/our lives. I feel like such a fool. We had so many close moments over the years. Although you are not physically present, I know you are still present and with me in spirit every day. I think of you often and of the wonderful part of me and my family's life you are. I miss your hugs and warm presence. I am so proud to say I am a part of your life and you are a part of mine and Christian's. We are so fortunate and blessed. You are like a son to me. Thank you for all that you are!

Garrett, please forgive me for not listening more closely when I SHOULD HAVE. You know, the moment you were speaking to me, I SHOULD HAVE paid closer attention. I SHOULD HAVE recognized, I SHOULD HAVE taken action as a responsible parent, adult, and friend. For this, I will always regret and am deeply sorry. It was 1 week prior to your decision. I SHOULD HAVE!

You have taught me so much about life. I now listen more closely, so as not to ever say "should have" again. You've made me and many others a better person, but at a very high price!

I must admit, I was angry at you for a little while. Why weren't you more straightforward with me? Even though you knew me so well as a very literal person, black and white, needing things spelled out and put in my face, you held back and neglected to be obvious the last time we spoke. Or maybe, I neglected to really listen. Were you vague or was I ignorant?

Of all the friends of Christian's, or teenage boys for that matter, that I've ever met, you by far, were the most considerate of others, always and without fault. How is it then, you could be so "inconsiderate" of those family and friends that loved you the most? You ignored what really matters in life and it bewildered me for a long time. Finally, through realization of my own life experience I could begin to imagine the overwhelming fear you were faced with. Regardless of the consequences of impractical choices, life altering or not, everyone has that same challenge daily. Because of you, I am now much more cognizant of making decisions based on fear. The past is the past and none of us can walk back and change anything. The time we've spent together will always be treasured!!

When all is said and done, "This too shall pass." I can only try to look for the treasures in the trials and know that the journey makes us who we are and helps us get through it.

For all that read my sentiments written to a truly treasured, lost loved one, I would like to say this, "Nothing is so important in this world once the value of a life is recognized and considered!"

Garrett, you have the best of parents and family. I've always known this. They continue to be an inspiration to many. I will always look out for your mom and be there for both of your parents as they need me, you can count on that. Mindful of not carrying on, as you know me to do and were so tolerant of, the bottom line is, if I could take back one moment in time to help you and make a bigger difference, I would. If I could give you my life, it would be yours. I love you with all my heart and I always will.

Kelly

Hey Laurie!

Attached is my artwork that I made in memory of Garrett. What I will always remember was his humorous personality. It made people laugh and have a better day no matter what the circumstances were. Building that structure for our math class, playing video games, and our air soft tournaments will always live on as the good times as we grow older. How I wonder what it would be like if he were still here and the kind of person he would be. No matter what, all I could do is look back on the times I spent with him and smile because he had his way to remind me to not take life too seriously. Thank you Garrett for being a part of my life.

Love,

Jacob Byers

Illustration by Jacob Byers

Section 3: **FRIENDS OF THE FAMILY**

Suicide can create a domino effect of so many feelings. In this section, family friends express how Garrett's suicide stirred many emotions for them as they, too felt a sense of loss and tried to help the family and loved ones cope. This section expresses how people try to come together even during the most difficult times.

The one thing that I'm thinking about right now is that for weeks after Garrett's death, once I got over the initial shock, I would listen to "Calling All Angels" (K.D. Lang/Jane Siberry) every night in bed, with my iPad set on repeat and cry myself silently to sleep. It would still be playing in my earphones when I woke up in the morning and I would hate that because I would have to face again that Garrett's death was real. My husband asked me repeatedly why I was torturing myself. I felt for some reason I needed to. I loved Garrett, but I realized much later that I had been trying to somehow take on some of Laurie's hurt for her. If I felt it so deeply maybe somehow it would be less painful for her. Seems a bit silly now when I actually put it to words, but I guess at the time it was the only way I felt maybe I could help. I was feeling it as a mother of a son.

Love,

Shari xoxo

I gave this a lot of thought and then never wrote it up.

I think of a great family always on the go. I think of loving parents that would do anything for their kids. How I always felt your family had it all together.

I think of one of the most exciting hockey games my kids participated in.

I was so sad to hear. It makes me sad to think how he could have thought that was the only way out when he had so much to look forward to and such a loving family. Drugs do that. Drugs ruin lives.

Love you!

Janet

To Kailee, Laurie, Tom and Chantal,

I hope everybody is doing extremely well!

First off, let me preface this by saying what you are doing is benevolent and wonderful. I'm sure I'm not alone in expressing my wonder at your courage and generosity in putting together a project like this. If even only one lost soul feels like they are not alone as a result, I could think of no better legacy for Garrett to leave.

I have had the pleasure of knowing the Savoie family as a result of one of the most important friendships I've ever had or will ever have in my life, with one of my favorite human beings, Kailee Savoie. Naturally, I spent a lot of time at Kailee's house with her and her family growing up. Kailee and I used to put a lot of effort into getting on Garrett's nerves. We'd say it was because we were bored, but I suspect this is how pre-teens and adolescents can still keep their siblings involved without admitting they actually like them. Garrett was always just in the next room with a friend, across the dinner table, or quarreling with us over whose turn it was to use the computer or watch the TV. When the adults would say something silly over dinner, we would all meet eyes and roll them in unison, united momentarily in our youth and the fact that we knew everything.

November 18th, 2010 was my 21st birthday. I woke up bright eyed and anticipatory, ready to answer all the birthday wishes and celebrate a milestone with my friends and family. I logged into my social media accounts and checked my phone, ready to feel the warmth of everyone's wishes. It did not take long to read about Garrett.

I don't remember particularly through what channel the news reached me, but I know I learned the information through written words because I had to re-read them several times. Even then, it still took a minute just to comprehend the symbols. I sat back and looked out the window. I did not want to celebrate my birthday anymore. I felt heavy and disturbed. I felt ashamed of how silly I had been a few minutes earlier, so presumptive that birthdays were just something you received yearly and always.

Mainly I was incredulous and frightened. Incredulous because Garrett taking his own life did not seem like something that would happen in a sane universe. Frightened that it might actually be true, and further still, scared for my friend. The thought of the pain she was undoubtedly feeling at that moment pierced me straight through. I still consider Garrett's passing with a devastated sinking feeling and the confusion still lingers.

I am the youngest of four children and have had a somewhat turbulent relationship with my two eldest siblings, in particular my eldest brother, who has always possessed a volatile nature. A small secret part of me has always feared that suicide was something he could be capable of. When I met with my family later that day for my celebratory first legal drink, I stared at everybody a little longer than necessary, drinking them in instead. I laughed at everyone's jokes too long, hugged and touched and poked them an unwarranted amount of times. They probably thought I was just tipsy, but I didn't mind. I threw my brother a few sidelong glances. I don't think he noticed.

I spent the most time with him that night. I forwent the option of leaving my family to be with my friends, and stayed with my siblings as long as possible. My brother lingered the longest, and we shared a night of hilarity and ridiculousness. Today is August 20th, 2013, his birthday, and I have just finished laughing with him over the phone, so intensely grateful he has had another birthday. Garrett reminds me how important it is to tell the people you love just that--that you love them and they matter.

It's not always possible to convey those feelings. Sometimes you are separated, whether by oceans or resentments, time or fear. These things are nothing, and they change nothing. Love is love, and the loss of a beloved person creates a myriad of profound consequences. If anyone needs proof, look at Garrett. I couldn't even begin to explain the magnitude of the significance his life had. People he may have never imagined would be hit hard and forever impacted by his departure. His existence was and is incredibly astounding and the hole he left behind is infinite. I wish he had known how important he is. I wish he was still just in the next room.

I hope this was long (or short!) enough, and I hope it's along the lines of what you need. Please don't hesitate to let me know if you need more or different information, or really anything at all. My love to the whole family.

With love,

Gia

Laurie,

This is such a deep subject that shatters all of our defenses. I can't help but think that it was a momentary irrational urge, the reason for instinctively not wanting to go near the edge of a cliff because you're afraid some unknown impulse will make you jump. It feeds that fear in all of us that we are capable of acting in ways we would regret. The reality of consequences beyond that moment don't exist.

We are all joined at the spiritual level and it wreaks havoc with the soul when one of us gives it up. Although I didn't know him personally, he was still "one of mine."

This book is good. It takes us past what happened to what can we do about it. This loss of life has made me feel closer to you than ever before, but at the same time, more distant because the pain of the reality is always there and we humans do so love to avoid pain.

Let's get together.

Lori

Hi Laurie,

I have given a lot of thought on your request and have had a lot of trouble thinking what to say.

At the time when you told me about what had happened I was so upset for all of you and really upset for you on how you found Garrett.

When this happened, I was still spending time looking for and finding Jay in some terrible places and conditions. It made me think how that could happen to me and question if I could ever be as strong as you.

You are such a strong person and, so I believe, all of your family. So what I think about is the strength of you and your family and how sad I am that Garrett didn't see that in time. I do think about Garrett when I think about you.

Not sure if this is what you are looking for but they are my thoughts.

Love you bud....

Barney

I didn't know Garrett and yet his life and death had a profound effect on me. I met Laurie when my oldest and her youngest daughters rode horses with the same trainer. As our friendship developed, Laurie became aware of parenting struggles I was experiencing and, with her own life experiences, shared her story so that my path may be a bit easier. She left the door open for me to contact her anytime. I called her from time to time and we met for lunch to share concerns and parenting strategies. I received unexpected calls from her to touch base and assess ways she could help. We shared a deep commitment to guide our kids through their "tough adolescences."

I was horrified for her and her whole family when I learned they lost their "G-Man". The pain I experienced resonated, recalling conversations of concerns and tough decisions. I was sad and had a sense of hopelessness.

Listening to Laurie speak at Garrett's service made an incredible impression on me. Her inner beauty permeated the room. There was a double rainbow in the sky as the service came to a close. I will never forget that day.

The profound affect I referenced evolved from hopelessness and fear, to be a return of hope, a strengthened faith, and a running tally of my grateful list!

I am grateful Laurie is my friend. Laurie's heart has **amazing** capacity to love. She is harnessing her grief to help and heal herself and others, a positive growth experience, born of her son's passing. It will make a difference!

He must have been an incredible kid. Even though I never met him, Garrett has meaning in my life.

I found this note and wrote it on an angel for Garrett's tree:

We're given many gifts as we go through life. Some we're allowed to enjoy for a long time, others only briefly. But each gift has the capacity to change us, enrich us, and make us better people. In your sadness, may there also be joy that you had such a person to love.

Author Unknown

"God grant us the serenity to accept the things we cannot change, courage to change the things we can, and wisdom to know the difference."

Love,

Amy Cummings

Here's a Find the Word Puzzle for Garrett's book.

My feelings and thoughts are hidden with the puzzle.

A	F	G	N	R	Y	B	L	O	H	G	F	Z	C	O	U	R	A	G	E	O	U	S	V	T	Y
N	S	K	Y	M	K	P	O	I	R	U	Y	T	R	E	W	Q	K	M	L	P	O	U	Y	F	H
F	G	H	J	K	L	K	O	E	S	D	F	G	H	J	N	N	T	E	A	R	S	S	V	N	P
G	H	U	M	J	O	L	P	I	I	N	J	U	H	B	V	W	E	E	R	T	T	E	W	A	E
F	B	J	U	Y	T	L	F	A	A	C	D	E	R	T	L	O	V	E	V	G	Y	H	J	I	A
R	T	Y	H	N	E	M	K	U	Y	F	D	W	E	E	R	T	Y	U	P	O	L	K	M	N	C
I	D	R	T	H	Y	Y	U	I	O	L	D	S	L	A	Q	W	S	D	C	V	F	F	G	B	E
E	D	R	E	W	A	Q	W	E	R	F	T	G	G	I	J	P	L	K	N	B	V	C	Z	X	F
N	C	V	S	S	M	A	R	T	C	V	B	N	M	J	G	J	I	K	O	L	G	H	T	B	U
D	K	P	O	I	U	Y	T	R	E	W	Q	D	S	D	G	H	N	M	T	R	B	H	M	N	L
K	K	F	E	T	A	S	D	F	G	H	K	L	L	O	P	M	T	N	B	V	G	A	C	X	Z
T	Y	U	I	P	O	L	O	P	A	K	J	H	G	F	D	S	A	Z	X	C	V	P	B	N	M
A	A	S	D	F	G	X	**G**	**A**	**R**	**R**	**E**	**T**	**T**	X	Z	S	D	R	T	Y	U	P	M	N	B
L	O	I	K	M	J	U	Y	H	N	B	G	T	R	F	V	C	D	E	W	S	X	Y	Z	A	Q
K	L	G	U	A	R	D	I	A	N	O	F	C	H	I	I	L	D	R	E	N	L	O	P	J	M	N
W	E	R	T	Y	U	O	I	K	M	L	P	I	J	U	H	T	F	R	D	X	C	W	C	V	B
C	F	T	Y	G	H	U	V	B	J	I	M	K	M	N	H	Y	T	R	E	D	F	Q	I	A	C
B	H	H	B	N	M	M	O	L	J	U	H	N	Y	G	C	X	A	N	G	E	L	X	Z	T	V
V	B	E	H	H	Y	U	W	U	I	Y	G	H	S	J	K	L	M	Z	A	Q	W	S	C	B	H
X	Z	W	A	E	R	T	Y	H	R	T	Y	F	C	S	V	D	X	F	C	X	P	V	B	G	N
Z	D	F	G	V	H	Y	U	J	Y	M	K	I	O	L	Y	M	G	Q	W	E	U	R	O	T	S
U	Y	T	G	R	E	W	A	S	D	F	G	H	J	K	L	O	L	P	O	I	R	D	U	Y	O
K	U	I	O	L	Z	N	C	V	B	N	K	H	G	F	D	S	U	E	R	T	P	T	T	Y	N
V	H	J	J	K	L	J	H	I	U	T	F	R	E	W	A	S	D	F	G	H	O	H	J	K	L
X	S	A	V	E	D	X	C	V	B	N	M	K	I	U	Y	G	V	C	D	E	S	R	T	Y	U
L	I	U	J	H	R	T	G	B	B	R	O	T	H	E	R	L	K	U	T	G	D	J	V	B	N

Love you,

Maria Williams

We met the Savoie's at the school bus stop in Tatum Ranch. The kids were picked up early every morning attending the local elementary school. This was the time I met Garrett. He was a cute, soft- spoken young lad. I remember him as a bit shy and reserved, but active with sports, camps and other activities with his friends. There were many kids that used to play in the neighborhood. They would run around outside playing in the cul-de-sac, screaming, yelling, chasing each other, laughing, having a great time. Often, they would end the day jumping in the pool to cool off, looking for a beverage and a snack, typical, normal kids having a blast. As Garrett entered his teens, his love of hockey and video games was evident. He would always be in the driveway practicing his shot, honing his skills. Garrett's parents being Canadian, playing hockey was a given. His dad had the love of the sport and always supported Garrett's participation.

When I heard of Garrett's passing, I was shocked, sad, and asked myself, *Why????* He had a normal childhood, loving parents and every opportunity ahead. What I realize is that when we lose loved ones young or old, we always have a difficult time accepting the loss and it often becomes time of self-reflection for family and friends. I only can imagine the difficulty of losing a child. My mother always said that she wanted to go before any of her kids. It would be too traumatic to lose one of her sons.

My thoughts and prayers will always be with Garrett and the Savoie family.

Garrett was a kind, gentle young man and we will all miss him.

Paul Ortman

I believe you meet people in your life for a reason, and sometimes you meet the wrong people, because you choose the wrong path or it's because of the moment. And sometimes, these wrong people lead you to the right people in life. Although, I will never really understand why we have to go through life meeting the wrong people, especially those that have done you wrong, lied to you, cheated or were just spiteful towards you and maybe even lead you down the wrong path. Some people only think of themselves, do not think of how they will affect others, and don't care if they take advantage of others, hurt others and cause harm for their own benefit. These people I believe have bad karma and will continue to their entire life. As you get older, you start to realize that you have no time for the wrong people in your life. It's sometimes hard to get these wrong people out of your life, too. You never know who you are going to meet along the way. You hope only to meet good people.

I was traveling to Kelowna, BC, Canada. I was at the Phoenix airport at the gate and this is where I met Laurie. We were both traveling to Kelowna to visit family. We were able to get together during our stay in Kelowna and the more and more I spent time with Laurie, I realized that she was a really good person. We became friends and once we returned to Phoenix we made more and more effort to be friends. Laurie opened her heart and shared more about her family and the tragedy of her son, Garrett, committing suicide. My first reaction was how could this happen to Laurie and to her family? Why would Garrett do this to her and his family, to his dad and his two beautiful sisters?? But mostly, to Laurie? I didn't even think about Garrett's reasons, just why would he do this to his family?

In the short time that I became friends with Laurie, she was there for me. She would go out of her way to be my friend in so many ways. Laurie is a true friend. I wish Garrett was here for her and her family. I wish he didn't commit suicide. It really makes me sad. Although I didn't meet Garrett or know him, I've gotten to know of him through Laurie. I admire Laurie and how she deals with her son's suicide, her kind words about him, her devoted love for him. Although Garrett isn't here physically, through Laurie he is here spiritually. I can see her sorrow sometimes and I wonder how she and her family manage to deal with this every day.

Garrett's suicide affected so many and as Laurie's friend it affected me.

Sometimes, sad and terrible things happen to really good people and it has a rippling effect.

You meet people for a reason. I met Laurie at the right moment and I'm very grateful to have her as my friend.

Sandra L Berault

When I heard of Garrett's passing, my heart ached. I was skimming through Facebook and WHAM - saw the post that caused a huge hit of overwhelming sadness. Only a parent can know the painful feeling when your child is suffering. When our children suffer, we suffer. The best way I can describe the emotional pain is to say that it turns into physical pain and it seems as though you can actually physically feel your heart ripping open. And after Garrett was gone, I felt that ache for Garrett and his family. Perhaps the intensity of it was because I have so much respect for his parents. The Savoies are special. I have always admired and respected the love that they share, the happiness they get out of living life and their kind and embracing hearts. Although I don't see them often, and I only met Garrett one time, the Savoie family holds a special place in my heart.

Every thought I have of them is either one where they are imparting wisdom or enjoying themselves and the people around them. When I think of Tom and Laurie, I immediately smile and feel good inside.

After learning that Garrett was gone from this earth, I couldn't sleep. As I stared sleeplessly at my ceiling, my thoughts were of Laurie and Tom and of their pain. How could two people who love each other so beautifully, love their children with all of their being, two people who have given their children an incredible life--make sense of this? How could they find a peaceful place in their minds that would allow them to move on? And as my thoughts moved to my own family and my own children, I looked for ways to find some guidance, some kind of message, from Garrett. It was that thought that spurred me to take a good look at my own family, my own children, and my own approach to family. And the thing that kept rising to the top of my thoughts was this one thing--life moves fast and we can give our children everything--yet the way they feel is up to them. Their perception of the world is just that...theirs. We can only do our best to show them the good in this world and teach them to be confident. Yet, the decisions they make are up to them. With that being said, I stopped to check myself and really ask the hard questions: are we enjoying our life enough? Is my daughter's view of herself and the world around her the best it can be? The truth in my answers were "No." More sleepless nights. I took it from there and am making sure we have more fun in our home and have improved the way I parent so that I can give my girls every opportunity to live confidently in this world.

That is the gift I took from Garrett.

I also want to add that I am soaking up the wisdom and strength I am observing (through Facebook of course) from Tom and Laurie. They have given all of us who know and love them a tremendous example of how to live life, how to find strength when energy is depleted, and how to honor their son by sharing their courage. I cherish their example.

God bless.

Debra Bernoff

When I heard the news about Garrett, it was complete shock and disbelief. Mainly because of the kind of loving, generous and caring people I know Laurie and Tom to be. Being friends with Laurie you immediately see how much she loved her kids with everything she had. My one major thought regarding Garrett's suicide was that if this could happen to this family, I absolutely know it can happen to anyone. I immediately wanted to go to Laurie and just hug her. I had to get to her as soon I could, but I questioned bringing my teen son and daughter with me to see this woman I knew was heartbroken and in anguish, someone they knew. I didn't want to scare them. But I decided they really needed to come with me. They should be there as support, comfort, and to see for themselves the devastation suicide has on those left behind and to be aware of this especially at their age, for their own sake and for the sake of their current and future friends in case they were to ever encounter someone who mentions or implies that they would want to hurt themselves. I know my kids will never forget going to see her that day. This is a very sad and tragic event, but to happen to such a family makes it even harder to accept. My heart still aches for them. Garrett's picture from his memorial remains on my refrigerator to this day. Even though I did not personally know him, I know Laurie and he was a part of her and Tom. His picture with his bright, beautiful smile is how I will think of him. This family will always be in my prayers and I admire and praise their courage and goals to make something good come out of this sad event. If anyone can do it, they can. They will always have my love and admiration. I know they will see Garrett again.

Cindy

Hi Laurie,

I am having a hard time with it! Mostly because you are such a good friend and I care so much for you and because it digs up old feelings from my past. I just don't know how to put it in words and I do not want to hold you up! I will see at some point if I can and will write you a personal letter.

I am so sorry, Ann

Section 4: **FAMILY FRIENDS MEMORIES**

Many people rely on memories to help them cope with a difficult time. Suicide is one of the most difficult deaths to accept and rather than focusing on loss, many people choose to remember a time when that person was happy and whole. In this section, family friends discuss the memories that they have with Garrett and his family.

Laurie and Tom and family,

I have spent the last 2 months thinking and processing the information in your letter because I didn't want to just contritely jot down something without pondering the meaning of why such a tough subject as death is so difficult to address, for me. But it is. It leaves me speechless, powerless and completely paralyzed in response to the loss of loved ones, much less a close friend losing a child. It's so hard to talk about Laurie, as I am only speaking for me right now.

I have found an excerpt of some things I have been reading over the past few months about Divine Enlightenment which you, Laurie, and I have shared many times when we talk, since Garrett has passed on. This stood out for me in how I would describe the kind of people you are as a family and how your imprint on me and my family will last a lifetime even if we don't share any common interests, per say.

"It is by divine design that you don't know the mission you signed up for---you don't need to know it to live in the godly ways that make a monumental difference! Beloved family, you do more than make a difference, you ARE the difference! As you lighten the lives of others, you also exemplify the innate strength and courage that evokes the determination and confidence to successfully deal with challenges. You benevolently influence others simply by who you are--by your very being, you are a rainbow of hope and a light to others!" Author Unknown

What I wrote above is for you, Laurie and Tom and daughters, to read before I give you what you ask of me and family to put in your book to help other precious souls who are struggling in this physical world. Here goes...

In reflecting on this, I was at work two days after my 50th Birthday, when my husband Ross called me to tell me what happened. I have known Garrett since he was about five years old. My daughter, Taylor, spent all her elementary years with Garrett and his sister, Kailee. Since we lived in the same neighborhood together, they also took the same school bus every day, shared many birthdays, trick-or-treating on Halloween night, and family events for over a decade. Garrett was very athletic and hockey was his sport. He was quiet at times, but always had a warm smile whenever I saw him and enough energy that would light up a city. He was a very happy child and I admired how Laurie would have so much patience and interaction with him and her daughters and their home was like a Montessori school--tons of activities and arts and crafts to do. I learned a lot from the Savoie family on how I could raise my children with the joy, fun and carefree interaction she did for hers. I never knew a mom so enthusiastic about raising kids! Fast-forwarding to the present day almost two and a half years later, I continue to experience regrets on how I could have better comforted the family survivors of Garrett's death. All I felt when it happened was anger and rage about him taking his own life because I knew how it would impact his entire family and beyond. There were so many acquaintances that the family had built over the years-- sharing their lives with us, sharing their bountiful generosity with us and their community was huge. All of them reflected the same energy and I'm sure some still enjoy the Savoies as we did and still do today. I think often still how I could have done more to have gotten to know Garrett better, maybe experienced a more closer connection with him, perhaps impacting on his earlier days more profoundly so that I wouldn't feel the regret and guilt of neglecting to do so--the "shoulda, woulda, coulda" scenario.

He is so very missed by me, my children and husband. It's a myriad of endless feelings that just don't go away, ever. Each of my family members deal with the different layers of sadness, loss and regrets as well. My greatest sadness is that the dynamics of my friendship with this beautiful family has changed, not because we wished it so, but just because it *is* no longer what it used to be. What connects us now is the pain and loss that we didn't share before. What I grieve now is what we had before it all.

The profound emotions that surround us now after this human loss has given us greater understanding of how much we can honor and respect the joys and deeper connection to the people that cross our lives and make it count. This is something I have not been aware of until now and this awareness has helped me see what I need to change in myself and something I will share and teach to my children and extended family and friends.

I hope this serves the memory of Garrett's passing and helps in your endeavors to help others who struggle with the thoughts of suicide.

Such a difficult subject to address, but glad I did.

I love you guys and cherish our memories forever!!!

Love,

Shirley Ortman Daniel

Hi Laurie,

What a worthwhile and brave undertaking this is for you and your family. I'm sure you still seek to understand and perhaps people's input and insight will help in some way, both for you and the others you envision reading this book.

I had just a few interactions with Garrett, both at his home and at mine. He was always kind of quiet, polite and seemed to me to be very close to his sisters. Garrett brought Chantal over to ride horses one afternoon. He did all the chores happily, had great patience with Chantal and enjoyed his ride in the arena. Again, he seemed very devoted to her and was very good with the horses. He had a natural ease with them, although I knew he hadn't spent a lot of time around them. I was comfortable with him handling them.

When we heard the news about Garrett, I was shocked and in disbelief. He seemed like a regular kid--riding the bus home, hanging with friends and doing his chores. I didn't know him well enough to know he was troubled, but in the few times I was around him, I never suspected anything was different about him. I understand that the circumstances which may have led to his decision were made a while after I saw him last.

Garrett's death has certainly been with me ever since. I was heartbroken for all his family and often think about how everyone is healing and coping without him. Hope this helps a little Laurie.....

Best to you all,

Love,

Barbi

My son Keegan had the pleasure of playing ice hockey with Garrett from 1997-2002. Good times were had by both boys and dads playing street hockey on the Cave Creek cul-de-sac for a few years as well. I remember that Garrett loved hockey as much as we did and had an enormous amount of energy. Hockey was a bond that both Tom and I had with our sons and something that can never be taken away. There is not one time when I watch a hockey game (which is a common occurrence) that both Garrett and Tom don't cross my mind. A good boy, Garrett will be always missed by Keegan and me. Although Keegan is now at ASU and I only see him once per month, I look at the missed opportunity that both of them could have played club or men's league together. I miss him and look at my life with Keegan and cherish whatever time we have that much more.

I will give him a BIG HUG in heaven.

Love ya' Man,

Peter Leary

Hi Laurie!

I've been thinking about your request to contribute to Garrett's book. I think it's a great idea! As a teacher, the most moving effect was listening to other teachers who knew Garrett as a young student. Listening to them describe his great potential, his character while at school and the loss they felt from being dedicated to him and his learning was very sad. Most simply felt awful. It's hard for teachers who serve as guides to problem-solving accept that they lost one. Garrett definitely made an impact throughout his life. Best of luck with the book. Take care,

Cindy Brown

Hi Laurie,

What you are doing in Garrett's memory is wonderful. I think of you and your family so often with hope for your, Tom's, Kailee's and Chantal's healing.

Although I've known and understand loss and grieving, I can't possibly begin to understand what Garrett's death has meant or how it has affected you. I do know how it makes me feel and I ache for you.

It seems as though for everyone growing up is challenging. In today's world, however, I believe it may be especially difficult even for one who is well-loved with so many influences, so much pressure.

I clearly recall the rainbow as I was leaving (still teary eyed) after your very moving memorial for Garrett. Since rainbows are even less frequent here than our always welcome rain, I felt quite certain that it was a sign that your son was now at peace.

Linda McCarthy

Hi Laurie,

Here is mine and my dad's entry. Miss you guys and hope to see you all soon! Thanks for letting us be a part of this.

Lindsay

Dad's entry:

When I think of the saying, "Life is a vapor," it makes me think of Garrett's life. Way too short. We know Garrett had so, so much potential just by looking at his two amazing parents and sisters. I had the privilege of living in your guesthouse for several months just before Garrett's death. To be so close to such a wonderful family dynamic and to see the generous spirits of all the Savoies, it was beyond heartbreaking to receive the news of his suicide. I, along with so many people, have been forever changed and encouraged by the Savoie family's unconditional love, hospitality, and kindness. I will always hold a place in my heart for Garrett and know his legacy will live on through Tom, Laurie, Kailee, Chantal, and many others. Leave it to you all to use this tragedy for healing and encouragement to so many people.

Love,

Michael Stream

The Savoie family holds a special place in my heart. Garrett played an extremely memorable role in my childhood. We lived in the same cul-de-sac in Cave Creek. With a contagious laugh and zest for life, any interaction I had with him brightened my day. Kailee and I were best friends and I'm sure obnoxious as all get out, but Garrett would join in the fun and never became annoyed with our ridiculous activities, ranging from making commercials, eating a whole box of otter pops, karaoke (Shania Twain). He had a gentle spirit I can recall vividly. He was also insanely good at hockey! ☺ He was truly a kind soul, much like the rest of the Savoie family. I have always been inspired by the way in which the Savoie family regards all people, no matter who they are, with genuine respect and care. Life will never be the same without Garrett here on earth, but I know he has left an extraordinary legacy through his family and friends. Many have already been changed and I know many more will be impacted by Garrett's story. Can't wait to see you in heaven, Garrett. It is comforting to think that Garrett no longer experiences pain and suffering and to think of him smiling down on us all. Love you Savoie family. Thank you for your bravery in sharing your families' experience! We never know whom we may encounter on a daily basis suffering from emotional/physical pain. Someone may be in desperate need of hearing Garrett's story and sharing it could save lives.

Love,

Lindsay Stream

Garrett Savoie

As I stood in the middle of our brand new cul-de-sac in the fall of 1998, I met Tom and Laurie Savoie for the first time. I still remember details of that day and our first conversation. Laurie and I were both expecting new babies, so thus began our instant connection and bond. We talked about how exciting it was that we would be neighbors and how much fun it would be to have our babies play together in the future. Tom also was excited about their recent move from Canada and the love he had for Arizona already. We talked about when our house would be finished and the excitement of our kids all being so close in age. We loved the idea of them being able to play together in such an amazing neighborhood in Cave Creek, Arizona. I sensed a sincere warmth and kindness within Tom and Laurie already and couldn't wait to live within a few feet of them. Neighbors, though I didn't know then, they would soon become dear friends!

The next three years would be a treasured time for our family! We were so grateful that the Savoies were such a big part of that time in our life. Garrett was around seven years old when we first moved in. He was this precious little blonde spitfire that never stopped moving. His hours of street hockey in our cul-de-sac were so much fun to sit and watch. He was passionate and always wore a beautiful smile. He was friendly and never hesitated to volunteer if anyone of us needed help. He was a smart, friendly, talented, and tender young boy. I instantly loved Garrett and his two sisters. His older sis, Kailee, became my daughter Lindsay's very best friend and they played together every day. Even though Garrett was the younger brother, Lindsay and Kailee always enjoyed playing with him in endless games, skits and swimming in the pool. Hours and hours of laughter, growing up just as children should, surrounded by love, fun, parents that adore each other, siblings, amazing neighbors, and then more hours of laughter.

Tom and Laurie were and are such great parents. Often referred to as Saint Tom by all of us neighbors, Tom would walk in the door from a business trip and start helping Laurie right away. He would play with the kids for hours and was such a great and fun dad. He also did laundry, dishes, housework and never hesitated to give Laurie much needed nights out. He adored Laurie and his children and showed it with actions and words. Some of my best memories are of watching Tom interact with his son, Garrett, playing street hockey and other active games out in the cul-de-sac. I loved the way Garrett would smile with joy as his dad would reiterate to him how great he was playing. How proud he was of Garrett. How much he loved him. His only son and pride and joy! Laurie was just as amazing as Tom. She never wavered from her love for her family, showing it with being involved in every aspect of their lives. She volunteered at their schools, took them to sports, lessons, activities, and everything they were involved in. She cooked perfect balanced meals every night, helped kids with homework, swam with them in their backyard pool, and still made time for date nights with Tom and game nights with her children. More than all of that, Laurie loved unconditionally. She never missed opportunities to show and tell her family how much she loved and adored them. She was an amazing example to me in every way.

Little did our family know that in fall of 1998, we would meet a family that would impact our life in so many, many ways. Throughout the next 12 years, we would sometimes live states away from each other, but always stay connected as good friends. We celebrated all of our children's successes, whether it be a graduation, a new job, or anything that they were experiencing. Our happiness was watching our kids grow up. Tom and Laurie had much to be proud of, two beautiful and smart daughters, and a handsome, smart, compassionate son, all three full of life and dreams.

Nothing could have ever prepared me for the phone call that I received on a cold November day in 2010. I remember falling onto my bed sobbing trying to wrap my brain around what my husband was saying. He told me Garrett was gone. He had died and was gone. He had committed suicide. As Michael's voice shook with the news, I cried and begged for it not to be true. Garrett was so young, so full of potential, so full of life. He was turning his life around. He was doing so much better, even working at a landscaping job that he loved, and spending more time with his family. How could his parents endure such a loss? How could his sisters ever go on? How could all of his dear friends understand this? How could we endure this kind of pain? How could I tell my children in the next room? How could I tell Lindsay, who grew up with Garrett, playing with him almost daily? I couldn't stop crying, wailing into my pillow, begging God for this to not be true. *Please God don't let this be true*. But it was, and Garrett was gone. Garrett was gone no matter how much I prayed and begged, he really was gone. I knew God had him in His care now, and that Garrett would never feel pain again. This gave me comfort, though I still couldn't stop hurting, crying and just trying to make sense of this. How could I pick up the phone and call Laurie? I was numb, but had to pick up the phone and call right then. I couldn't wait...

We cried and cried and cried some more. I will never forget the sadness and emotion in Laurie's voice in that moment, the despair of a mother who had just lost her child. A mom who would give her life a million times over for any one of her children. A mom who had just experienced the greatest loss any mother could ever face. She had lost her baby boy, her precious Garrett. I will never forget that moment for the rest of my life.

The truth is there is no sense to be made of this. Suicide is something that everyone I know has been affected by. The only common denominator that I can come up with is pain. The pain becomes too great and the quickest way to end the pain is to end life. I can't imagine the kind of pain Garrett must have been in, but I do know this, if he had felt what the rest of us feel about him, he would not have ended his life. He would have known that his life already had made a difference and had impacted those around him in such positive ways. He would have known that his parents would do absolutely anything to help him. He would have known that he had way too much life to live and too much to look forward to! He would have known that few sons are as treasured by his family as Garrett was. He was loved by all! He was someone who had support, prayers, and unconditional love from his family. He would have known that the hole left in their hearts would always stay empty. Nobody could ever replace such a vibrant, loving and amazing young man. He would have known that, but in a moment in time, he forgot or didn't realize that, and ended his life.

The following are 3 reminders of Garrett in my life:

A quote, a song, and a poem...

This quote is a reminder of Garrett.

"If ever there is tomorrow when we're not together...there is something you must always remember. You are braver than you believe, stronger than you seem, and smarter than you think, but the most important thing is, even if we're apart...I'll always be with you." -(Winnie the Pooh)

The song that I hear on the radio and at church that always reminds me of Garrett. It's by Chris Tomlin and is a version of *Amazing Grace*, which I love.

My chains are gone

I've been set free

My God, my Savior has ransomed me

And like a flood His mercy reigns

Unending love, amazing grace

The earth shall soon dissolve like snow

The sun forbear to shine

But God, Who called me here,

Will be forever mine.

Will be forever mine.

You are forever mine

And lastly a poem that reminds me of Garrett's parents, Tom and Laurie--not that I would ever even pretend to know how they feel or even what they have been through.

They tell me it's amazing how I've stayed so strong,
but they don't see how I cry when I hear your song,
they see the smile on my face but miss the hurt in my eye,
I would rather seem rude than let them see me cry,
I put on this front as I don't want the world to see,
the pain and sorrow so deep inside me.

I don't act this way cause I'm ashamed to feel the way I do,
I act this way in honor of you,
because although I hurt right now and my heart is broken,
I can't help but feel pride and love when your name is spoken,
my strength comes from the love you gave to me,
and it's that strength I want the world to see.

I will always love and miss you Garrett,
that I will never hide,
and when people ask me about my son Garrett,
they will always see my pride,
you were so precious and your memory will always live on,
I'll never be sad that I had you....
only that you're gone.

Dedicated to Tom, Laurie, Kailee and Chantal Savoie
In honor and memory of Garrett Savoie

Love always,
Kerry Stream

Hello Friends:

It is with a heavy heart that I come to write these words. While I certainly feel sadness of the loss of a wonderful individual, I also feel privileged to have known him for the short time that I did. Everyone we meet in our lives touches us in some way that we often don't understand at the time-- occasionally subtle, and at times surprisingly profound. Garrett Savoie is one such individual. Having known his parents since my own teen years, I was aware that Garrett grew up in a loving home with extremely strong family values. I truly never worried much about his future as I could not imagine a more nurturing environment. That stated, it appears that God (or whomever you choose to believe in) has a more mysterious plan for us and our loved ones.

In thinking about destiny, I often ask myself; what good could possibly come from a situation like this? There appears to be no justifying the loss and suffering that the family has to go through and the loss of potential. Perhaps it is not within the scope of my understanding to comprehend the meaning behind this loss. Nonetheless, I have a lingering feeling that I am supposed to learn something and take something from the moments that I knew this young man.

Upon further reflection, I began to realize that the messages are perhaps more simple than I initially perceived. Quite literally, Garrett reminded me an awful lot of myself at that age. He was a combination of gentle com- passion for others and a troubled self-doubt and tendency toward over- judging oneself. Perhaps my knowing Garrett was a message to approach life with confidence and self-assurance and worry less about what others think. Maybe it was to see hope in his youth and be inspired by that, for life is fragile and cannot be taken for granted.

Regardless of the complex messages we are supposed to take away from knowing Garrett, there are some memories that are much more accessible and offer a smile. Garrett was a playful and friendly young man, always ap- proachable and willing to offer his million-dollar grin. Despite his troubles, "G Man" (as many of us knew him) presented himself as positive and upbeat. I also remember his energy as a young boy. He had a truly insatiable appetite to move and be active. If only I could possess a small portion of that energy.

I feel as though my life has been enhanced for having known Garrett and writing these words makes me realize that even more. The world lost a valu- able asset when we lost Garrett. Too young and way too soon. Thank you Tom and Laurie for allowing me the opportunity to have known your son. I will always consider him a friend and I will not forget him. God Bless you.

Kevin Kasper

Garrett Savoie--a beautiful, warm, and kind young man.

It seems just like the other day, we remember spending an afternoon with Garrett and his family celebrating his high school graduation. He had the kindest smile, warmth of a little boy and excitement of what awaited him in the years to come.

We will never forget that incredibly sad morning. We were shocked and instantly felt so much pain; that immediate pit in our stomachs can still easily be felt today. Our first thoughts were to run to the family, love and hug them and somehow make all their pain go away.

Then reality set in, the questions of maybe it's all just a big mistake. Then total chaos set in and all the questions. *Oh my God, how are Laurie and Tom holding up? What about the girls? How can we help them? How can we turn back the clocks and make everything better? How can we take some of their pain away?*

We only wish we would have said something to Garrett or done something for him to influence a different outcome for his life.

Later that day, driving to the Savoie home in a state of shock and daze, I witnessed the cars passing us by, the kids on the school bus and people jogging. My immediate thoughts were how is it possible for the world to be going on as normal as if nothing happened? Damn it!

I got angry and truly felt the world needed to stop! Everyone should be grieving the loss of this very special, beautiful, warm, kind and loving, son, brother, grandson, friend and young man!

We can only hope you were lucky enough to have met Garrett.

Jeanne Bernard

Hi Laurie and Tom,

I know I told you I'd write something for your book, so here goes! I really didn't know Garrett as well as others have because Kailee and Liz hung out with each other, but here are my thoughts.

If you were to ask me what I remember most about Garrett it was his beautiful smile and laid back demeanor. Any time we came to visit, or you came to our house, he was always smiling and in a great mood. He was quieter around us because we didn't have any boys for him to hang out with.

The one thing that stands out in my mind happened one night when you and Tom went out to dinner and our daughter, Alexandra, was babysitting. After TV and playing, she put Chantal to bed and Kailee was up in her room listening to music and doing homework. It was after 9pm and Alexandra told Garrett it was time for bed. He said no. Now we know that most kids don't like to go to bed so she let him stay up another 45 minutes or so. Finally, she got to the point where he refused to go to bed, and I still find this hard to believe, Alexandra put Garrett into a headlock and said you need to calm down now and go upstairs to bed! He reached around and slid out of her grip then turned and punched her in the stomach! She started crying and called us. I went to your house and found her crying and Garrett up in his room with the door locked. After Alexandra stopped crying, I told her she shouldn't have gotten physical with Garrett and if he got up and came downstairs to call me. Garrett never came down, and the evening calmed down.

The next morning, you and Tom came over with Garrett and he apologized to Alexandra and us saying he was sorry and he would never do that again. His apologizing showed character and we were touched.

When I think about what happened that night, I realize that Garrett had a strong spirit and didn't want to listen to authority like most young teens. Garrett definitely had strong beliefs in what he thought he could do. We are certain that he is having a ball on the other side, being creative, smiling and really enjoying the work that God called him to do! He is forever a part of our family and he joins all the other young people that God has called so I'm sure they are all having lots of fun. Having also lost a child, we can only believe that they were called for a purpose that is hard for us to fathom and when the time is right we will be with our children again and have lots to talk about!

Laurie, I hope that what I wrote is okay. Never been part of a book, but it's something that I remember about Garrett!

Love Mary

I can't remember the first time I met Laurie and Tom Savoie, but I came to know them best when Laurie was Shannon's Girl Scout leader. Laurie led the troop from first through fifth grades for Shannon. With her easygoing personality, Laurie always made everyone feel comfortable. She had something fun and creative for the girls to do at their regular meetings or took them on special field trips. It was such a fun and learning experience for these young girls and their parents. Laurie had the energy and the imagination to get the girls excited about being Girl Scouts.

One day when I was at Laurie's house, I noticed a chore chart on her refrigerator. She was so organized and had her kids helping her with chores daily (something I've always struggled with). I only met Garrett a few times, but he struck me as a well-mannered, handsome young man. I was impressed that he volunteered his time to help special needs children and adults through horse therapy. Disciplined and caring would be two qualities that I would equate with Garrett from my viewpoint.

When I heard that Garrett had died and was no longer with us, I couldn't even imagine what Laurie and Tom as well as Chantal and Kailee were going through. Many people struggle to understand why bad things happen to good people. The only way I can deal with it is to give it up to faith and turn it over to God. I'm praying that we will understand the whole picture at some point in this physical lifetime or in our spiritual lifetime. Meanwhile, we continue our journey on this earth and remember our loved ones who have passed, knowing that they are still part of us – in our memories, thoughts, and actions. And live with the hope that we will be reunited with them at the end of our life's journey.

Julia Smith

We have known the Savoie Family for many years and as a result have had the blessing of being able to get to know and love their children.

The good memories are plentiful with both Laurie and Tom, Garrett, and the girls, Kailee and Chantal. Our visits to Calgary when Garrett and Kailee were babies and Chantal, just a twinkle. Your visits to our cottage in Northern Alberta and ours to your Phoenix doorstep.

The boys had lots of fun with Garrett. He had such ZEST and ENERGY, and a smile that lit up the room. We used to tell him how much he reminded us of his Grandmother Joan - mischievous, kind-hearted, and always up for fun!

He introduced our boys to paint balling and helped them expend a ton of energy, particularly with the "sprinkler under the trampoline trick". We even brought that one back to Canada. Outdoor hockey day and night to the disdain of the CRANKY neighbors. "BRING IT ON!!!!" Mom Laurie would say, and of course the boys, "they did".

Over the years all the kids grew and we saw less of each other, but always stayed in touch. And then one very sad day we heard that Garrett had taken his own life. THIS BROKE OUR HEARTS. So final and such incomprehensible grief that I knew Garrett would never have wanted his family to experience this, he must have just run out of answers and did not know where to turn.

We think of him often, especially our boys, as they now experience the pains of growing up and the learning of their own independence.

Garrett is our light and reminds us to never, ever give up. He makes us smile when we think about his precocious spirit and he keeps us going when we have lost our steam.

Thank You, Garrett, for giving us that strength right now.

We love and really miss you! The Loney Family.

Section 5: **THE IMPACT OF SUICIDE**

The impact of suicide is something that is very apparent once it becomes a part of your world. However, many people may be unaware of that impact simply because they have been fortunate enough to be spared of such a tragedy. The words offered in this section focus on the deep impact that suicide has on those who have been touched by it and how that impact touches the rest of their life. While a person can certainly learn to cope with suicide, once it touches your life, it is a part of you forever.

Dear Tom, Laurie, Kailee, and Chantal,

I thought that the best way to remember Garrett, for me, would be to use excerpts from the message that I wrote for his memorial service. I pray that this is a help and inspiration for you and others. I pray that it helps point everyone to the truth that there is hope for life in Jesus Christ.

In His peace,

Pastor Paul Witkop, *Light of the Desert Church*

The apostle Paul compared our lives to a race. Toward the end of his own life, he wrote, "I have run the race, I have finished the course." All of us would hope that our race is a marathon. As we gather here to remember Garrett, all of us agree that Garrett's life seemed like more a sprint that included some pretty high hurdles at the end. James compares life to a vapor, here today and gone tomorrow. Every day is a gift—and what God calls us to do is to receive each day as a gift and live it to its full potential.

So today, we are here to remember Garrett's life. In the midst of our remembering, we are here to acknowledge our loss...and to find peace and comfort and to begin the healing process. A week ago, none of us would have ever dreamed we would be here. I know how much Tom and Laurie and Kailee and Chantal and the rest of Garrett's family and friends appreciate your presence, your love and care.

We are most importantly here to receive the healing that God can only bring---that comes from hearing and trusting his promises--- and it comes from sensing his love in each other.

So many of you have expressed very well what Garrett was like. He was a young, energetic, sensitive, caring, young man with a terrific sense of humor and —who loved his family very deeply. He loved high energy activities like hockey and snowboarding and paintball.

He was a committed and caring brother who always told his Mom—love you mom! He felt things very deeply and sometimes had difficulties expressing what he was feeling. In this past year, he especially enjoyed his joy at Arizona Plant and Landscaping Center. Tom and Laurie told me that this job that included working with his hands and being rewarded for his excellence with new responsibilities... was something that Garrett really loved. It was a huge ray of hope in what was a very difficult year.

It's very natural for us to ask God how Garrett's tragic death could happen. We will never fully understand…. because we were not walking in his shoes—we all see the world a little differently. We like straight forward explanations, but often, in life, the answers are not simple.

Tom and Laurie shared with me that life was tough for Garrett, especially in the last year or two. Though he was much loved and loved his family very much, he was looking for his place in the world, and learning how to deal with freedom and pressure. He was making some good progress—working to beat his challenge with drugs -- but in the end he also made some bad costly choices. These choices were not the Garret we remember. And, they certainly don't reflect what God wants for any life.

God's desire for all of us is to live a full life, confident.

- That we are loved by God,

- That He has a purpose for us,

- That we can trust him in any situation

- That we walk together with others who love us and know the same.

But, we also know that all of us have sinned. None of us are perfect. We all lack faith, at times. So we need help. We need a Savior. That is why God sent his Son, Jesus, into the world to die on the cross, to pay the consequences for our destructive and sinful actions, to give us hope for our life here and for eternity. And though we tend to run away from everyone in tough times, He wants us to know that He is there for us even in those darkest times. Where is God? God is with us. He wants us to trust him.

We read from Romans 8 where the Apostle Paul reminds us that if God is for us then it doesn't matter who is against us. *Nothing can ever separate us from the love of God*—not even the worst catastrophes of life. God's love is a free gift that we receive by faith.

Paul says it this way, I AM SURE that nothing can separate us from God's love.

Jesus said to his friend and he says it to us…, *"I am the resurrection and the life. Those who believe in me, even though they die, will live, and everyone who lives and believes in me will never die. Do you believe this?"*

God wants us to know that there is more to life than 20, 40, 80 or 100 years on this earth. And God created us to live here in a relationship with him and then to enjoy an even closer relationship with Him in eternity.

<u>What can we take away from this day?</u>

• Treasure each day---embrace life fully

• Love your family and friends

• Life is way too short to hold grudges or to hold back forgiveness.

• Make the right choice. We can become bitter or we rely on God and grow better.

• Reach out to those who are in need. The lonely and those who are looking for direction.

• Most importantly, <u>trust your life to the one who gave his life for you</u>—Jesus Christ--- no one loves us more than He does.

• Remember each other in prayer, but prayer is action as well. Give a call, a hug, and a visit.

• Ask God for his peace that surpasses all human understanding.

Thank you God, for your peace and for all these people who have come together to be a blessing to each other. Thank you for our time with Garrett. Thanks for your love that is greater than everything. May your light shine brightly in the midst of our challenging times. In Jesus name, Amen.

I remember the day Garrett left this world very clearly. Although Phoenix Fire Dept. Crisis Unit is dispatched on many suicide calls, this one was special! I will never forget the look in Laurie's eyes when she asked me, "WHY?" I so wish I had an answer for her! On every call this question is asked. The answer lies within our loved one and we truly can never know for sure! But while we have the chance, let everyone know how much they are loved. Also, that there is always hope that tomorrow will be better. We may not get a second chance!

Love and many blessing to you and your family!

Pam - *Phoenix Fire Dept. Crisis Unit*

I wish I didn't have a reason to write this. I wish I was writing a congratulatory speech at Garrett's college graduation or at his engagement party or birthday. Not for this.

I don't remember the first time I met Garrett. He would have been in elementary school though, because that's when I met his older sister, Kailee. I went to her house for a playdate and met her siblings and parents for the first time, not thinking much of it. I'm sure Garrett was playing video games or something else that I had no interest in as a pre-teen. He was always around, trying to annoy us. I never really talked to him, he was just my best friend's little brother.

Then Kailee left for boarding school when we were 16. I didn't get to say goodbye. I didn't get to talk to her on the phone for months and months. It was really hard. Then Garrett and I were in the same chemistry class junior year and I naturally latched on to him just for news of Kailee and to be near someone with her same quirks and traits. It was as close as I was going to get to have her back for a while and I enjoyed spending time with him. He was a total goofball, but he was a sweetheart. Then the year ended, more time passed, Kailee came home, we graduated and went to college and I only heard bits of what was going on with Garrett. I knew he was partying more and into drugs, but I had no idea how bad it had truly gotten. And I didn't find out until it was too late.

I opened my messages one night and saw one from Kailee. All it said was "Garrett killed himself last night. I'm coming home tomorrow. I'll call you when I get home". That short message changed everything. I couldn't understand how or why this happened. I re-read the message multiple times and realized what I was reading. I was in shock. I didn't know what to do. I couldn't call Kailee. I felt really helpless. I called Kailee's parents to offer to pick her up from the airport. When her dad answered, I told him that Kailee messaged me and asked if I could do anything. Then he asked if I was okay. That was when I started crying. This man had just lost his son and here he was asking if *I* was alright. That's the kind of family Garrett had.

The next day when Kailee got home she called me. I was in the shower, but heard her ringtone and answered anyways. She updated me on what was happening, and what had happened. When she told me that her mom got to the hotel right after it had happened, and was the one to find him, her voice broke. I tried to keep it together and told her I would be there soon.

As soon as we hung up I started sobbing uncontrollably. Just imagining Garrett in that situation, making that decision, his mother having to be the one to walk in the room and see what had happened– all of this just broke my heart. I was crying so hard my roommate had to come in and check on me.

I cried the whole way to their house. And as soon as Kailee walked out and hugged me reality finally set in. I didn't know what to say so I just hugged her, putting as much love into it as I could. The house was packed with people. There was enough food brought over to feed an army. So many people just trying to help in any way they could, but knowing they could never do enough. We didn't talk about what happened. We just made plans and drank too much wine, trying to forget why we were there.

The funeral was a haze. I couldn't tell you what was said or what songs were played. When they asked people to come up and speak if they felt they needed to, I walked up there without really think-ing about it. I had no idea what I was going to say. The most important thing was letting everyone know how great a person I thought Garrett was. And I reminded his family how much I loved them. I really wanted to make sure they were hearing that. Later that night, Kailee's parents each pulled me aside and thanked me for being there for Kailee, but they didn't realize that being there with them was what I needed, too.

As time went on, I worried about how everyone was doing, espe-cially Kailee being back in Canada at college and not at home with her family. When she came home for Christmas, I was just wait-ing for her to break down. After a few days, it seemed like all our friends assumed she was doing fine, but I knew it was coming. And one night after we went out she finally let it out. I stayed in the bathroom crying with her for over an hour. I had nothing to say but "I love you" and "I'm so sorry" over and over and over again. I knew I needed to say more, but I couldn't. It hurt so much to see her like that. I don't think she knows how much I worried about her. How often I thought about her. I wanted to make sure she was alright, but if she was I didn't want to bring everything back up. I had no idea how to handle the situation. So I just let her bring it up when she wanted to. I hope that was enough.

It's hard to know what to do when something like this happens. You can't plan for it. And everything is so fuzzy and your emotions are all over the place. I went from confusion, to sadness, to so much anger, to even more sadness. And once the grief passed, the worry for his family set in. Things got more stable, but they'll never go back to normal. I think when Garrett made that decision he thought it would be the end of things. But it wasn't. It never is. He put his loved ones through a hell one hundred times worse than he could ever have been in. And I know with all my heart that Garrett never meant to hurt anyone. But he did. He hurt a lot of people. I want to go back to the last time I talked to him and shake him and make him see what he was doing and how he could stop all of it if he just asked for help. But I can't do that. I can't do anything to ever bring him back. If I could talk to him again, I would tell him that I love him. And I'm glad he's happy now. Oh and "high five" (Borat voice). Miss you, kid.

Kelcie W.

Hi Laurie:

It is very difficult for me to respond to you regarding Garrett's untimely passing. It moves me so deeply as it brings out so many emotions such as anger, sadness, and yes, happiness knowing Garrett. As you know, Stewart, my brother, passed when he was young. This is not like a suicide, but unexpected as well. I like to think that I know a bit about what you went through after.

The stages of grief are overwhelming but I think we tend to get "held up" for a number of years in some of these stages. With my dad's death five years ago, all I think is, *here we go again,* and I seem to be stuck still in the sadness phase a lot.

Garrett was a very large part of your lives. Yes, being the only male like my brother was, makes it even harder to get through the emotions. I know exactly the "mother/son" bond and even though we love our daughters, still something is truly missing. When I came to visit you with Tracy over six years ago in February, I got to know Garrett a little better. He was vivacious, loving and truly cared about all of you by the way he spoke and treated us respectfully. So when I heard he took his own life, boy was I mad!! That subsided into disbelief, then sadness, asking why, and now talking helps with the grief.

I use to hate when people said "Time heals" or "We all are here for you" because really, no you are not!!

But actually, all those things are true, you just don't want to hear it so soon. Sometimes, we need our grief and need to wrap the sadness around us like a warm sweater just to begin to heal.

The girls miss their brother terribly so, just like Tracy and I missed Stewart. At first, we thought we could hear him call our names or see him on the street. Often, I found myself picking up the phone thinking I need to call him for advice, but then realizing he is not there. That's good to feel that way because it means I have not forgotten how big a part of our lives he truly was. Conversation helps. It makes you remember, but sometimes makes others feel uncomfortable. Good friends understand your need to talk.

I have an old saying I got from my grandmother, "Be properly preoccupied with life". When I asked her what it meant she told me, "Laugh often and as hard as you can, love with all your heart and if you lose, lose with grace knowing you are that much smarter and you lived well." Some wise words. Often, what we say to others can hurt, but owning up to it makes you a better person.

Sorry for rambling on. Hope this bit of input helps you see a bit of my side of the fence. Thank you, Laurie, for sticking by me by including me in your friendships by sending me a birthday card (thanks!!) and keeping in touch. God has a special place in heaven for you!

Love, Cindy

Dear Laurie,

First of all HELLO!

I received your letter in the mail and I am, once again, amazed by your strength, kindness and thoughtfulness. Your family has been through so much and here you go again pushing forward thinking about and wanting to help others. What an honor for me to know you!

I wrote a little something about my experiences that I have included below. I am not good at putting my thoughts into writing so please know that I *do not* expect you to use this in your final piece! It is yours to keep, re-arrange, change and do whatever you feel necessary.

Most of all, I wanted to express my love for you and the pain that I felt for your entire family and our community with the loss of your precious son. I am so proud of you for creating such a heartfelt project to bring people together to discuss such an important topic and to also open the eyes and hearts of others in the future to prevent another tragic loss.

Sending many blessings and much love to you and your family, Laurie! I hope to see you soon.

Love,

Suzanne Spellicy

When thinking about the tragic loss of Laurie's son, Garrett, two similar incidents come straight to my mind.

My first experience with this type of death was as a sophomore in high school when a classmate committed suicide. My feelings of sadness about his death were geared more toward his siblings since I could relate best to them being of that age and having brothers myself. I felt extremely frightened and depressed about this loss and it made me very confused not being able to understand why or how this could occur in such a young boy.

My next experience with this type of death was in my early 20s when my high school boyfriend (and prom date) committed suicide. We hadn't had much contact in the recent years prior, but the emotional pain of his loss was still there. Our childhood memories and the feelings of young puppy love were just overwhelming and the broken heart was felt. I thought about the fact that we were just reaching the age of adulthood and we had so much to look forward to in this life.

This leads me to Laurie. I met Laurie when our kids attended Desert Willow Elementary School at the same time. Laurie was in the school parking lot each morning to greet the parents in their cars and to help our children safely onto the school grounds. She was such a ray of sunshine and a joy to see each morning and we became friends. I will never forget the morning in November when we pulled into the parking lot and Laurie wasn't there, but her volunteer partner quickly told us the tragic news about Laurie's son, Garrett, passing. My feelings went straight into "mommy mode". He is her son! I have two sons! The immediate heartache I felt for Laurie, as a mother, hit right into my soul and has never left. I honestly have no words to describe my aching feeling.

All three of these experiences in my life have been young men who grew up in extremely loving and wonderful families and environments. I cannot pretend to understand why or how a young man can end his own life. I just know that the pain they must harbor and endure saddens and frightens me. This must be the pain that we all feel after they are gone. I truly wish they were able to know the number of people who love and adore them and how the love for them trickles out and touches a countless number of people that they are completely unaware of.

I am deeply sorry for the pain and emptiness that so many people have experienced in the tragic loss of Garrett and I pray that these real stories can help prevent this type of loss for the future.

Suzanne Spellicy

Puzzles and I have never gotten along. My sister, who is truly gifted in so many ways, purely ROCKS at puzzles. I missed that part of our genetic code and have often found myself completely helpless to finish one stinkin' puzzle. To make it worse, if I ever do get to the very end, that memorable last piece, the trophy part itself is typically missing. Missing!

How the heck can you finish a puzzle without the last piece? Where is the joy at the end? Where is the sense of accomplishment that all of your hard work, your diligence, your precious time completing the puzzle matters?

A family and the community in which it lives is a puzzle. Each piece fits together forming a whole. Every person is an integral piece connecting one piece to the other making the puzzle strong. One of the worst things that can happen in a family or community is for a person to be lost from that whole.

If even one piece is missing, the puzzle will never be complete. In fact, the pieces around it are more likely to fall off, too. The missing piece makes the whole more fragile. The connections that were once so strong are now weak. The puzzle is no longer a whole, but fragmented.

Losing someone to suicide is the ultimate missing piece.

When I heard about Garrett's choice to take his life, I was just about to welcome some eager, bright smiling faces into my home. One of the many joys of my life is teaching preschool. The children I teach are full of life. Their joys are simple--an ant walking across the sidewalk draws wonder. The wind blowing the leaves of a tree illuminates their faces with a smile. The tenderness of a new idea sparks their curiosity and opens their minds so easily and so openly. I love teaching preschool and love this beautiful age of innocence. They are fresh, new puzzle pieces....

But on that morning, I could not even open the door to welcome my first eager student. As the first parent opened the front door for me, she immediately saw the ache and pain on my face. Her bright smile dropped and thankfully she turned to the others as they were walking in and said, "Something has happened and Kristin needs us to turn around today and check in with her later."

You see, the sweet, eager smiles slapped me in the face that day as the horror and pain of a family I loved dearly clouded any happiness I saw. My first reaction was to do something, so I prayed and I prayed hard. I asked God to guide my ways. This tragedy was bigger than me and I needed a power that could not be broken. Dang that missing piece!

Missing pieces do not mean to go missing. Sometimes they just get lost.

When a puzzle is created, every piece is fresh, unharmed, unused...new. As people start manipulating the pieces, they often will show their wear. Maybe they were not treated so kindly. Maybe they were dropped, got soiled, got trampled. Maybe they were forgotten and found later on. However, if all the pieces are still included the puzzle still creates a masterpiece.

Later that day, I went to the house I had been to many times before. Ironically, it was not Garrett that I knew very well, but the love of the family he was a part of that I had come to cherish--his family's puzzle. You see, sometimes you do not need to know each member well, to know that when one is gone, nothing will be the same. It is that loss that aches your very soul.

What I did know of Garrett I saw in the bright eyes of his mom, the pride of his dad, and the smiling faces of his sisters. I heard countless stories of his zest for life, his boundless energy and contagious humor. I saw pictures of his beaming smile and knew how easily it captured the hearts of those around him. Many times I was able to witness those smiles for myself and my heart grew for this child of God.

I also was privy to another part of Garrett's life through stories his mom would share. How he struggled to fit his unique perspectives on how things appeared to him and how they appeared to others. How his life was an uphill battle at times. They were stories of challenges and hurdles, stories of choices that were caustic, and stories of exertion to no avail.

At times, he was a tattered piece, but until his fateful choice that day he still made his family's puzzle complete.

Garrett could not have had a better family. He was loved beyond measure and cared for with the love of many. The Savoie family does that to people. They draw you in and keep you as one of their own. Once you are privileged enough to enter their hearts you become a part their puzzle too and their puzzle has many pieces.

Losing someone to suicide is the ultimate missing piece.

When Garrett died, the puzzle he was a part of started falling apart. Remember what I said about puzzles, once one is missing the connections are fragile. The pieces of his family were the first to go--the puzzle pieces of Laurie, Tom, Chantal and Kailee were hanging on to him to make them whole. The emptiness of his piece was now making their connections very weak. They were at risk of breaking their bonds as well. They were left dangling.

A dangling piece has two options. The first, and most tragic option, is that it will just fall, become forgotten, and be lost itself with the horrifying chance of being yet another missing piece. If it falls, it too creates a hole and the puzzle one by one. The family, the community in which it was once a part of, may slowly begin to crumble, too. A missing piece has that effect.

Suicide is the ultimate missing piece. Dang, that missing piece!

In fact, many families crumble after losing someone to suicide. Their foundation is just not strong enough to sustain the emptiness left by the missing piece. One by one they fall, lost and misplaced. They lose sight of the whole, the masterpiece, the beauty of what it was once like to be a part of something bigger than themselves. It is a chain reaction that is tough to stop.

Fortunately, there is another option for a dangling piece, but it takes time, courage and the strength of all the joints around it. A dangling piece can be hoisted up, dusted off and placed gently and carefully back with the rest; joining it once again to the pieces that make it strong. It can remember that it too is important. It too may not go lost. It has a job and that job is to continue to be created as part of a whole.

Missing pieces do not mean to go lost. They just forget.

At this particular moment, the strength of the other pieces of the Savoie puzzle has held them together. It is my belief that God will continue to put people in their puzzle box that will help bind their pieces and hold them tight. It will take all the pieces of their puzzle to remain attached if they are to stay put. The emptiness will always be there.

A missing piece destroyed is not replaced. It is up to everyone to make sure their binding is tight and that, if they ever dangle again, they are pulled back and gently reminded of the masterpiece they create. The Savoie family has a strong bond in the people that love them.

But what of Garrett's puzzle? Not the one his family made around him, but the puzzle his life had not even begun to create? That is where the true tragedy of suicide lies.

A missing piece abruptly stops creating.

In this life, Garrett will never know what it is like to be gently put back into place. How it feels to be dangling, but then rescued and reminded of the importance of being part of a whole. He no longer has the ability to see that he made a difference. That he was an integral part of something bigger, stronger and larger. He misses out on seeing his masterpiece.

Suicide tragically ends life's creation in one single decision.

What will you choose? Will you choose to finish your puzzle? Will you choose to struggle through, build connections, strengthen bonds, and allow the other pieces the gift of holding onto you and bringing you home?

If you were part of my puzzle, that is what I would wish for you. I would not care what you look like, what scars you have, what rips and tears you show. I would want you, your piece, your beauty, and your bond. I would need you to make my puzzle whole.

Do not become a missing piece.

You were born new, fresh, and an essential part of something wonderful. You may be tattered, scarred, ripped and sometimes unrecognizable from that new piece you once were, but you are significant. You are needed. You are essential. You are a gift. Seek out others to lift you back in. Be patient, be courageous, be willing to ask for help. When you dangle, when you fall, find the strength to rise up and be found. There is a work of art being created right now all around you.

In fact, it is my belief that the biggest tragedy of a horrible situation is not the situation itself, but that people were not changed by what occurred. Garrett is forming a new piece right now in each of you. Use his memory to create a masterpiece, live bravely, and build a sturdy and beautiful puzzle. Let it be completed with you as the most important piece, the trophy, the prize, the infamous last piece!

Kristin S.

_____

I think the idea of writing this book is a good idea. I am glad you are doing this project and I think it will help a lot of people.

Personally, our family has known too many that have committed suicide.

Since our oldest son, Ryan, has been a freshman in high school we have known six that have committed suicide.

One was a girl Ryan knew in school. Ryan was real quiet about it. It upset the whole community and us as a family even though we did not know her.

Then, my uncle who was married to my dad's sister, who we were very close to, committed suicide. It was so upsetting and we were so in shock.

I had seen him just four months before he took his own life. My aunt and uncle lived in Las Vegas and we went to visit him. He seemed ok, but I could tell he was depressed. My aunt had died three years before this from an illness. My family was so devastated.

Three years after this happened is when I got the news about Garrett. Our friend, Lisa, called me that morning, and sounded upset. She could hardly talk and I was saying, "What is the matter, Lisa?" Then she told me that Garrett took his own life. I couldn't believe it. I was in utter shock. I asked her why and of course she could not answer that question. Our family had seen Garrett working at Jalapenos probably a few months before this happened, maybe longer than that, not exactly sure. He sat with us and we had a great conversation and he seemed happy. Also, we went to his high school graduation party and had a great time with him and everyone. So those were our last memories of him. They were good memories.

That whole day, I just felt like I was going to throw up and felt like I was going to pass out. I had to wait to call Dave, my husband, to tell him the news. I was crying too much and needed to settle down. He didn't take it very well and was very upset and angry at the same time. I was very upset and angry thinking, *how can anyone do this*? After my Uncle had done this, I never thought I would know someone else to do this. It is so shocking and upsetting to hear this kind of news. I get angry also, when I think about it. They do not think of all the friends and family and people they didn't know and how it would affect them so much. It affects us for the rest of our lives. I will never forget what happened. I still get depressed about my uncle and Garrett and the others that we know. I wish I could have helped them in some way, but we had no idea that these thoughts were going through their minds. Then my next thoughts were, *Oh my, how do we help all of you through this*? I just wanted to help in some way, to make the pain a little less, but there is no way to make the pain less. Just know, that we are there for you at all times.

The other three suicides were very upsetting, also.

One was an older brother of a friend of our daughter, Nicole, and we know the family well, also.

They had no idea these thoughts were going through his mind until after he took his life. He had just graduated college and had a wonderful life ahead of him.

Another one was also from our high school and had played on the basketball team with Ryan, our oldest, during their years at the high school. We found out he had been struggling with schizophrenia for a few years after this happened. He just could not take it anymore his parents told us. He felt like he would never get better. It was so hard to see all the basketball players last year gather at his funeral and say goodbye.

I feel like my kids have been to too many funerals already. They are too young to deal with this much loss.

The last one we know is from our high school, also. Davey, our son, is real good friends with the sister of the girl that took her own life. She had gone missing for a few days and some people found her. It was so sad to see it happen again.

I hope this book can help others from making this decision, I do not want to hear of any more people taking their own lives.

We love you all,

Lori-Anne Toomey

Laurie,

I have been writing and re-writing for months now. I didn't know how to put it in words and I didn't want to be selfish or not genuine. But I think this one finally sums up my feelings on it for me. You are welcome to use part, all, or none. I love you and admire your courage and faith. God bless...

I had not personally met Garrett and it's hard to explain the pain I felt as a friend of his mother.

The death of your child is your biggest fear as a mother from the first day you realize you are pregnant. You just want to get through the first trimester to make sure you don't miscarry, you worry still through the second trimester so you know they will be born with healthy organs, and even through their third trimester so they don't have to depend on science and doctors to keep them alive. We give up drinking, smoking, we eat right, we exercise, and we take prenatal vitamins. This is a gift from God and it is worth it.

This baby is born to us and we experience such joy and love that we have never felt before. Even when our second is born, we don't know how we could love another so unconditionally...but we do.

We stay up all night when they are infants worrying about crib death, we worry and watch them continuously as toddlers to protect them from electrical sockets and water and traffic.

We let them go to our school teachers, some we trust, some we don't. We leave them in sitters' care and worry constantly, but still try to have fun on our "date night."

They grow up to think they know more than we do, and we know it's our job to encourage them, but we still hover. We sacrifice so they can go to good schools, participate in sports, and excel in things they love. We stress about the kids they hang out with and the decisions they make.

We are proud when they obtain their driver's license, but then a new set of worry overtakes us.

We never stop worrying that one day fate will take this child from us. We cannot imagine the pain.

My friend, Laurie, and her family have had to endure this pain. No one can explain it, an explanation won't help. The pain I have endured on her behalf is minuscule compared to what I know she and her family have gone through.

I honor Laurie and her family for knowing that Garrett has served a purpose in his life here on earth. We know he is at peace and that Heaven is a better place since he arrived.

As difficult as it is to understand, God has his ways.

We don't know light without darkness.

We don't understand happiness without grief.

We don't cherish life without knowing death.

God bless you, your family and always..... Garrett Savoie

XOXO

Jeanette Laine

Dearest Laurie –

Thank you for your note to bring this back in front of me. Your letter came when I was on vacation and then our household move consumed the rest of my summer.

Ironically, I received your reminder email on the same day that I learned of a young man who took his life last week in the same way as Garrett. He is a family member of John's, a young man I only met once. John and I attended his memorial services this weekend and celebrated his life with his friends and family. Since I didn't know him personally, my grieving was not for the loss of his presence in *my* life, but for those left behind. I did not know Garrett personally, so I'd like to share my thoughts, feelings, insights, wishes and prayers for those he left behind; his mother, father, siblings, other loving family members, all his friends, and his community. I can only begin to imagine the pain and anguish of those closest to Garrett, each wondering what they could have – or *should have* done differently. Their pain, their grief, their anger must be simply overwhelming, and yet the person who took their life had no realization of what burden they were placing on those they love **because they were only focused on themselves at the time**. Those who are left behind live with an empty place that feels like a hole in their hearts that nothing can fill. *They are left with a haunting burden of not having been enough for the person that chose to die.* Those left behind feel resentment for the selfish act, and this resentment may even well up like a wave of anger and rage at times, torturing them with guilt and a feeling of hopelessness.

For anyone reading this book that has considered taking your life – please think instead, about those you'd leave behind. Think about those who love you deeply, even if right then you don't feel loving *toward* them. Be brave and ask for help immediately so you can find a way out of your pain, or desolation, or anger or desire for revenge. By reaching out and asking for support, you can get well and feel empowered again. Do whatever it takes to get back in the flow of joy. The wake of a suicide is an awful thing to leave behind as your legacy. Never think for even a moment that it's glamorous to be memorialized as a martyr by taking your life.

I can imagine that in some instances, one might also come to a place where they think suicide is their only option because they believe their loved ones would be 'better off' without them. Look into the faces of anyone who has lost a loved one to suicide, and think again. Your family and friends love you and want you here. No matter what struggles you are facing in your current circumstances, *they are only circumstances*... they are temporary, and they *can* change if you ask for help. You are here because God, the Universal Power, the Grand Order of Design, the One, whatever you call "It" – wanted you here to bless humanity with your unique and special imprint. Never give up. Live in the light of those who love you here on earth and never, never give up.

K. –

First of all, the Perez' commend you and your family for taking on this heart-wrenching endeavor. We never know how to deal with the death of a loved one until we are faced with it. Losing one's flesh and blood hurts more than losing a limb. I've been having a difficult time thinking of the right words without letting my tears get in the way. I can still remember seeing Garrett and Alex run around the neighborhood having fun without a care in the world. Then I remember seeing Garrett on his graduation day ready to take on the world. If only we could have seen his pain.

I've lost five other friends and family since Garrett's death, but his has hit home in a way the others couldn't. How I sobbed like a child, like never before. It could have been my Alex as they shared similar stories and upbringing. I could only imagine the pain Laurie and Tom must have felt if I felt the way I did.

I've also learned of the suicide death of two other CSHS graduates that following year. I still don't have a clear opinion or view on suicide, but what I do know is the pain left behind and how these demons possess them like a cancer. It takes over their life until the hurt is just too much.

My daughter said once, "Mom, sometimes the person feels that checking out will relieve them of pain as well as the pain they've imparted on their loved ones." Committing suicide, though a quick fix, leaves a wake of pain to those who are closest that will never pass, but hopefully eases over time. Garrett may be gone physically, but he will forever be with so many of us. What a great gift Garrett will leave behind. This book will help those that may have thought of taking their life so that they can see what is left behind.

Iris Perez

When we received the call about Garrett, in addition to the pain we felt for our friends of over 30 years, we were also reminded of pain we had experienced in our own family. The day before our wedding a young cousin (age 15) had taken her life and four months earlier Tracy's 22-year-old brother had been tragically killed in a car accident by a drunk driver.

The memories of the impact those events had on the families and the questions it raised has affected all of us. They have also become part of the fabric of who we are. Simple things like never hanging up the phone with our children without saying "I love you", being keenly aware of drunk driving and seat belt use. Simple things borne because of the too early deaths of people we loved.

Garrett's passing will have that kind of impact on those he knew, those who loved him and those who he loved. They won't be the same people they were before and overall that will be a positive that comes from this tragedy.

It seems trite to quote song lyrics, but suicide has often been described as a permanent solution to a temporary problem. The bigger problem is that the person contemplating suicide doesn't understand that those problems are temporary.

The song *Teach Your Children* by Crosby, Stills, Nash and Young might not be specifically about suicide, but the message is clear.

Communicate.

Teach your children that things will get better. They need to know. Teach your parents what you are going through. They need to know.

It is important and it will make a lasting difference. It is always better to learn from others' mistakes. We don't have to make them all ourselves.

The final message the song has for us is also important to both parents and children. If you remember that, all else is possible.

Tracy and Barry Carlson

Dear Sweet Laurie,

I got your letter and was stunned. I am out of the PVJR loop and had no idea that your son had died. I am so very sorry. A good friend of mine took his life four years ago. I remember where I was when I heard. I remember rushing to his wife's side. I remember all the details of flying out to California to bring their teenage son home from a school field trip and having the memorial service. I cried so much that first couple of years. We had over 400 people in our backyard for his memorial. How on earth did Matt not know he was so loved? My dear friend Matt was bi-polar. Much like how someone dies of cancer, he died from his mental illness.

I think I might have seen your son once in passing at your house. Although I didn't know him, from knowing you I know he must have had a big heart. Sometimes, those who love so much and well, feel pain with the same intensity. Garrett may have not had a long life, but he knew love. Some live their whole life never knowing the kind of love Garrett's family had for him.

I hope you continue on your path to healing and can get to the point where you can be joyful in your memories of your boy. My friend Matt and I remodeled my house together--so many happy memories of time spent together are in my house. I'm finally at the point where I can laugh about our adventures instead of grieving that we won't be having any more.

Peace be with you Laurie,

Xoxo
Susie Stelzer

Yes, please feel free to use my letter if you think it is a help to your project. I really did write it just for you :-), but don't mind sharing. I love that you are reaching out to others as you journey towards healing. I'm sure your book will be a balm on the hearts of many.

Xoxo,
Susie

...TENDER HEART...TORTURED MIND

In loving memory of a beautiful boy named Garrett and my colleague and friend, Kate. - by Johanna Renay

She loved wearing Chanel fashions. As editor-in-chief of a national publication she interviewed, attended media and charity events, lunched and dined, and sipped beverages with movie stars, politicians and people of note. She looked supremely self-confident, empowered and always moved with such wonderful grace and ease. In an industry where we couldn't/ didn't agree on much, we (her colleagues/competition) saw her as: sweet, kind, brainy, and beautiful (inside and out).

Her home life was full: 3 young sons, a medical doctor as her husband and a warm, supportive family of siblings, parents and so on. She seemed to have it all.

I admired her so much and always wished that I could be more like her: always calm, composed, and so very competent. She always seemed to say just 'the right thing'.

One night she checked into a hotel and having taken a cocktail of pills and alcohol went to sleep. She never woke up.

There wasn't even standing room as people filled up every nook and cranny available in one of the largest churches in downtown Toronto. And there was not a dry eye in the place either. We loved her and already missed her so much. And all we could manage to utter was, "Why?"

Watching the video of Garrett's 'celebration of life' was a deja vu experience--a beautiful and sweet young man with so much promise; with so much heart; with family and friends that loved him and believed in him and wanted to be there for him and with him for all of his life. Yet he, like Kate, made a 'choice' where the only thing that is left for us to say (with a very heavy and very sad heart) is, "Why?" And as Garrett's family puts it, "*...if love could have kept him alive--he'd be here today.*"

Written with much love for Laurie, Tom, Kailee, & Chantal.

We will always hold you all in our hearts and in our prayers.

Roy and Johanna

P.S. Thank you Laurie for involving me in this wonderful idea of yours. I believe it's people like you (and I adore you for this) who are going to change the world--one kindness at a time!

Upon hearing about Garrett's death, I immediately felt full of sadness for both his family, and Garrett. I feel sorry for Garrett because he did not think that his life was worth living and was not able to find help in time. I did not know Garrett personally, but I have become good friends with the Savoies and can tell how much they love each other. Losing anyone is such a horrible feeling and I cannot imagine having my sibling not be around anymore. Chantal is like a little sister to me and we have a great relationship. I am happy that she can come to me and talk about anything. I want to be there for her since her brother cannot at this time.

Suicide is a horrible thing and I do not understand why someone is willing to take their life. I feel no matter how bad a situation is, there is always a way out if you try. It may be hard currently, but in the end it is much better to fight to live than not. The Savoies are such an amazing family and they do not deserve this pain. Actually, no one deserves this pain. I feel that the Savoies have gotten stronger and continue to become stronger each day after Garrett's passing, but I can see that they have a part missing from their life. I am upset at Garrett for taking his life causing Chantal, Tom, Laurie and Kailee to have to go through this pain for the rest of their life. I did not know Garrett, but if he is anything like Chantal and his parents, I know that I would have loved him just as I love the rest of the Savoies. I hope that I do not know of anyone else that I know or that my friends and family know who killed themselves, the pain is too much and the people who want to take their lives need to realize that they are not freeing themselves from pain, they are creating pain. I hope that the Savoies continue to gain strength to continue to move on. I can imagine it is not easy, but they are an inspiring family and have shown just how strong they are.

-Ameena Arekat

Dear Laurie,

I start this letter by apologizing if anything I write causes any pain or discomfort as I will be as truthful and honest about my feelings and recollection of events that occurred when I heard of Garrett's passing.

I believe I was at home and had called DWES and was told of Garrett's passing. I did not know Garrett personally, but as I knew you, Laurie and Chantal, I remember thinking, *What? What are you saying? How?* I guess I was in disbelief and some form of shock. I then was told he committed suicide. When I heard suicide my first thought was*, oh how sad that he was in so much pain and could not see another way out.* Then I thought of you Laurie and how devastated you, Chantal and the family must be. I can still feel the sadness and sorrow that hits me in the pit of my stomach as I recall that day. I was thinking of the bond we mothers have with our children and how your world will never feel the same again. I was worried how you and your family would find strength and comfort with one another and not be pulled apart.

This moved me that night to hold my own children and talk honestly and openly about their own feelings and explain to them there are many options in life and that nothing is so great that it can't be dealt with. Garrett's suicide allowed me to talk openly and frankly with my own children and have them express how they felt about themselves, peers, friends and the world around them. I must say, it was surprising to hear all they had to say and I know it was due to Garrett that I could truly hear and understand all they were saying.

I am not sure at what point I heard of Garrett's history or struggle with drug use. This saddened and frightened me even further as I have many friends and family whose children struggle with drug abuse and see how destructive it can be.

I went to Garrett's service and as I was standing in the hallway and sitting in a chair I was listening to people talk about how Garrett's suicide had allowed them to talk to their children and face their drug abuse issues. As you stood up and promised Garrett something good will come of his death, I realized it already had. It gave parents the courage to talk openly about the issues they faced with their own children. I saw tears of pain and tears of relief as they shared their stories and found support in one another. You may not realize it, but Garrett and your family have touched many lives in a positive way. Garrett and the Savoie Family, thank you for sharing your story!

With much love,

Rose & Family

To whomever is reading:

My name is Mitchell McConaghy, a 23 year old student attending UBCO in Kelowna, British Columbia, Canada. I did not know Garrett Savoie personally, but I was a close friend and classmate to Kailee when Garrett passed and the feeling of utter shock and loss was felt by me and the entire campus community thousands of miles away from Arizona. When I personally heard the news from Kailee, disbelief was definitely the first thought I experienced followed closely by an intense bout of shock grief. It seemed like the day before everything around me seemed untouchable and then so suddenly my sense of youthful immortality seemed so stupid. It definitely made me put a lot into perspective. It makes you see just how valuable life is. It really made me realize that no matter how troubled you think your life is, know that you may be right, today life sucks, but tomorrow holds an unlimited amount of potential to change that. Seeing what Kailee went through the first year after Garrett's death, taught me so much about being strong, brave and determined in the face of adversity and I apply those lessons every day in life. I met Kailee's family and it reinforced the belief for me that when faced with a wall in life, a close-knit family can get though the hardest hardships and that love really does conquer all. I wish the absolute best for the Savoie family. You guys have been through so much and have been so diligent through everything. I have nothing but the utmost respect and admiration for you!

Thank you for allowing me to contribute to this book, I hope it helps ☺

Sincerely,

Mitchell McConaghy

I met Kailee in Kelowna, British Columbia when we were students at UBC. We had met in passing early in 2009, but began hanging out as friends in the two months leading to Garrett's death. Although I did not know Kailee very well at the time, this event affected me more than I could have imagined.

The night before Garrett's suicide, Kailee, some friends and I were hanging out in my apartment in downtown Kelowna. I just remember everyone having such a fun time, exemplified by the contagious laughter of Kailee and Mitch. The night ended as any other would, but the morning came with a profound impact.

Earlier in the day, Mitch had mentioned that Kailee had to go home – and it seemed urgent. Anyone's abrupt trip home would raise an alarm and since I didn't know Kailee very well I was concerned, but not speculating.

I remember walking in the door from school and heading towards my room.

Mitch said something along the lines of "I don't know if you heard, but Kailee's brother killed himself."

My stomach dropped and I didn't know what to say. I had been told of other people's passing and attended several funerals, but the news of a suicide felt very uneasy. I felt so bad for Kailee because she is one of the sweetest people I know and I just could not comprehend what she was going through. I didn't know the circumstances that had led to Garrett's suicide and I knew it wasn't my place to.

In the time that Kailee was back in Arizona, I, as a lot of us were in Kelowna, couldn't stop thinking about her and her situation proving the ripple effect that suicides create. You can try, and you can try to place yourself in someone's shoes, but at the end of the day only Kailee (and her family) knew what they were going through.

Now I can't tell how Kailee's friendship and mine would have grown had it not been for this tragedy, but I know that in the wake of it we became very close friends and I am thankful for that. We can talk about anything. The conversations that you are supposed to have in college regarding politics and innovation gave way to a much more real and impactful dialogue of life and death.

As any tragic death leaves questions, a suicide seems to leave an even bigger void. It was clear from my interactions with Kailee that too many things were left unsaid. I remember Kailee constantly questioning and apologizing if she were to tear up at seemingly random moments or if we found ourselves talking into the early morning. The fact is you cannot put a timeframe on an emotional recovery, especially on the scale of a suicide.

Now since Garrett's death in November of 2010, I unfortunately had another friend's brother commit suicide. I personally knew Curran and although we were not close, I again found myself constantly thinking about it and asking the same questions. A week before Curran's suicide, he was in my house at a Stampede pre-drink. He was cheery and lively. I definitely had no idea that in a week he would be gone. That next Friday, I opted to stay in, but would have been with him (as some friends were) in the hours leading to his suicide. I went to the funeral and it is unimaginable to see how many people cared for him and were grieving for him.

Now, it is hard to imagine the suffering that those like Garrett and Curran must have been going through to both consider and act on suicidal thoughts. If I could offer any piece of advice to get through to those struggling in similar situations it would be that "this too shall pass." Everyone experiences hardships, both in and out of our control. Our problems seem so consuming that we lose sight and feel alone as if we are the only ones struggling. Nonetheless, there is always someone who cares unconditionally for you, someone who is willing to listen and someone to find inspiration through on another path to happiness.

If these two unfortunate events have taught me anything it would be to always be conscious of the people around you. Everyone is fighting their own struggle whether they are showing it or not. Ask questions to those you are close to. If someone is acting out of character, question it and try to get through to him or her. Even if that person is just having a bad week, letting them know that you care will never hurt and just might help prevent a tragedy of the sorts.

Stefan

Garrett's Letter for the Savoie Family

I never had the opportunity to meet Garrett. I have never met his parents or his sister, Chantal. I have, however, met his older sister, Kailee and I consider writing this a privilege. It has been a privilege to know Kailee and get to know Garrett through her. I don't know if Garrett ever knew anything about me. It's a strange thing to wonder in hindsight, it feels pseudo-petty and self-centered. I know his favorite song and he may not have even known that I exist at all. What a strange thought.

I met Kailee when we were both in university. We were working part-time retail jobs and she was wearing a pink bedazzled sweater that would later become a topic of my many fashion-critical jokes. I don't remember what I was wearing. It's funny how you only ever really remember the beginnings and the endings of things because all I know is that from that day on we were basically inseparable. We did everything together, the dumbest, most ridiculous shit that twenty-year-olds think is grown-up. Nearly three years later, I still find myself regaling our adventures and laughing to myself. She'd joke that she was the "white chocolate" to my "milk chocolate" family. She was the best friend I could have ever asked for and we thought we were invincible. And for a while we were.

On November 17, 2010, I saw my phone ringing before I heard it; I was in the shower, mid-shampoo. To this day, I have no idea what compelled me to jump out and answer it, generally I could call Kailee back whenever. I couldn't understand her. I'll never forget what she sounded like though, and the only words I could make out: "Garrett", "my brother", "killed himself". I was out of my house before I could process anything. It had just started to snow at my house and it wasn't until I was waiting for Kailee on her porch steps that I realized I wasn't wearing any shoes and my normally bouncy curls were matted to my head with dripping water and shampoo like a wet Irish Setter. I remember not knowing what to say, I stammered something about being sorry I forgot my shoes and then just holding her. Everything else is a swirling blur of packing, phone calls, questions, and no answers.

Honestly, I thought this would be a lot easier to write. I thought I was more of a participant-observer and could just relay "the facts" and it took me a long time, even up until the point of writing this, to realize that I had a lot more insight on Garrett, Kailee, the events leading up to Garrett's death and the events following. I guess I never really realized how staggeringly angry and unforgiving I could be toward someone I'd never even met. I never tried to understand it either, until I actually sat down and tried to write this without sounding contrived. When I began writing this, I didn't see any possible hopeful way to end it. I was so unwaveringly angry at someone I didn't know for unknowingly taking away my best friend. Kailee changed so much. It made me feel so helpless, useless and fragile. Those feelings subsequently made me feel so petty, selfish and childish. How could I be so mad at her when she was suffering so badly? I knew the unfairness of the situation, but the unfairness of the situation in general was stifling. It still is.

On November 17, 2010, Kailee's parents lost their only son. Chantal and Kailee lost their brother. I lost my best friend. I miss her every day. That being said, I am so grateful that I was there. While I never had the opportunity to meet Garrett, I took care of Kailee to the best of my ability in this situation and considered her a sister. I know he would be so proud of the wonderful person she is. It has been an absolute honor getting to know Garrett through Kailee. I am so grateful for the opportunity to continue on Garrett's memory and the immense impact and significance of a life that touched so many.

-Jordan Knapp

LET'S BREAK THE SILENCE

I didn't know Garrett well. He was the high-energy kid of Tom & Laurie, friends I'd made in the mid-90s through my ex-husband, who worked with Laurie. We socialized infrequently, but always had much fun. Laurie and I shared a strong bond. And then the Savoies moved to the USA. We kept in touch at first, even visiting the family in Arizona where Garrett played "slide" down the stairs in their house with our daughter. (see photo) Time flew, and contact dwindled other than annual Christmas letters full of newsy family updates.

Fast forward to November 2010. I don't remember how I heard, or from whom, because all I felt was shock and disbelief!

Garrett, dead? Can't be true. How?

Apparently, suicide.

No way!!

Okay, now I have a dilemma... need to reach out to Laurie...but, oh God, what to say?

It would be easier to retreat in silence, thinking that in their grief, the family wouldn't even notice that I hadn't communicated, but that just didn't sit right with me. So I jotted some heartfelt words in a greeting card, hoping to convey the compassion I felt deep in my heart, but I knew those words would never be enough to adequately express the depth of the feelings I had for each member of the Savoie family, let alone acknowledge theirs. There really were no words to express the magnitude of shock, grief, and confusion. And I admit, I felt some fear too yet it was an underground anxiety that was inexplicable at the time.

About 18 months after Garrett's death, my daughter and I and some other friends visited the Savoie home in Arizona. The grief in their space was palpable, even though each member of the family was trying valiantly to carry on. And Laurie wanted and needed to talk. So we talked. And talked. And I listened. And we cried. And shared. And supported. It was awkward then because no one else in the house spoke. Everyone retreated into his or her own corner when Laurie started to speak.

And that inexplicable fear of mine reared again because Laurie admitted that she had always privately sensed that Garrett didn't belong in this world. Those words chilled my heart because I had often buried similar thoughts of my own daughter!

Fast-forward 14 months after that conversation and I had to agree to admit my daughter to the hospital's adolescent psychiatric ward because she had planned to kill herself. Truly, a parent's worst nightmare.

Throughout the ensuing shock and crisis-filled weeks, my thoughts and heart frequently turned to Laurie and Tom. I couldn't fathom how they had emotionally survived the aftermath of Garrett's suicide. The magnitude of their grief must have been unimaginable. Then and now.

Grief needs expression. Yet in our Western culture it's taboo to talk about death, especially if suicide is involved. Why is that?

I've thought a lot about the deafening silence that surrounds suicide and even mental health issues that often lead to suicide.

In our case, just this year my daughter was finally diagnosed with a genetic brain dysfunction (aka mental illness) that explains so much of her troubles over the years (and my inexplicable fear). She was first labeled "depressed" by a psychologist at age seven! At that time, we were given some parenting tips and sent home, never to speak of depression again until almost 10 years later when she was on the brink of making the same tragic choice as Garrett. In those 10 years, the number of different medical symptoms, emotional upheavals and numerous visits to various doctors and other health practitioners didn't result in anything but more confusion. And more silence. "She's fine. Her tests are all normal," is all we heard (with an underlying judgment that she was just a hypochondriac seeking attention). No one was connecting the dots because no one was speaking or listening to the truth.

Even my daughter! She had learned early on to hide her depression, to live a life of illusion, desperately trying to fit in, to appear "normal" when she really just felt "crazy". Even if she did speak her truth, she was silenced somehow. I admit it, by me too. It was just too difficult to accept that my beautiful, intelligent, capable child was not happy!! I also admit there were many times when I *silently* prayed that she would just "get it together" and choose joy over hopelessness.

Well, the truth of it is those silent prayers of mine, the judgmental glances by medical professionals and friends and family were felt by my daughter loud and clear! Which only served to deepen her sense of separation from the rest of the "normal" world, to deepen her depression and heighten her desire to depart the world that didn't hear her.

Our story has a happier ending than the Savoie's. When my daughter was in her darkest moment, diving off the cliff, I was beside her to hear her desperate and almost-final plea for help. And she got it, in the form of medication that has changed her world dramatically for the better. And as difficult as the experience was for her and her family, I am so grateful that she is not only alive, but thriving...at least so far. There are no guarantees, she has a mental illness that will stay with her for life. We can only give her the medical and emotional tools to manage it. But she was heard, and both she and I no longer feel any shame when speaking about mental illness and depression.

Was Garrett's fear and confusion buried in silence? Did he feel there was no hope of being heard, understood or supported? We will never know. I do know, from the bottom of my heart and soul, that he was loved and cherished by his family. Yet, he made a tragic choice to end his hopelessness. I hope and pray that his death provides all of us within the ripple of it's aftermath, with the courage to speak, to share our stories, to break the silence.

Depression is real and it affects our youth far more than we seem willing to acknowledge as a culture. We must take the cloak of shame away from an issue that has such dramatic and tragic outcomes if it's not acknowledged and understood.

Tom, Laurie, Kailee and Chantal...your courage in bringing this book to life is so admirable. It's tough, I am sure. You are going to have to face all the raw emotions you felt November 17, 2010 and thereafter. My heart bleeds for you. I can't ever pretend to know the depth of your despair, but I can offer my empathy and compassion to you, my shoulders to lean on, and most especially, my ears to listen. Speak. To each other, to friends and family, to anyone who will listen. Suicide hurts. And it doesn't have to if we as a culture embrace a more open approach to the reality of depression and mental illness and death itself.

When I was listening to Laurie speak last year, she brought out a box she was using to gather things in – snippets of memories of Garrett, notes from dreams and counseling sessions, and the like. I remember that she seemed afraid to bring the box out in public, that it was somehow a dark and shameful thing she was doing in creating it. But I also sensed that it was an important tool in her healing. And now I know it was a gift... to her, and to all of us in Garrett's ripple.

Barbara C.

The Uses of Sorrow

By Mary Oliver

Someone I loved once gave me

a box full of darkness.

It took me years to understand

that this, too, was a gift.

Garrett and Zoe

Cave Creek is such a community! We call it home and we see people we know everywhere. Often times, we feel like we know people better than we do because we see them at school, church, sports events and the grocery store.

I remember clear as day the morning I saw children sad and teachers with shocked faces. I asked someone what was going on. "Someone had died," was what I heard. "A sibling of a 5th grader," said another. Who, what, where, how and why? Eventually I heard that Chantal's brother took his life. "No!" I screamed to no one. Not another kid. Not that family. Not any family.

I walked into the school office and asked Jill if it was true, if Chantal's brother took his life? Her face and answer said it all. I began crying uncontrollably. I had never met Garrett and I barely knew this family, but a young man was so sad that this was the only way out. This tore me to the core.

It took me several minutes to control myself and to begin to imagine what Laurie and Tom were going through at this moment. Memories of young Chantal flooded through me and how her life was forever changed. Tom and Laurie's life had changed too. *Why? How? Why did God let this happen?* There were no answers only prayers for the family.

The days that followed left an empty place in my heart. I did not even know this boy. Why did it affect me so internally? Suicide is a permanent solution to a temporary problem and this tragedy of taking one's life needs to be stopped. The people left behind are the ones who suffer. Garrett has eternal peace and rest, but his family, here on earth, suffer. They suffer daily. They struggle with the why, how and what for. Sometimes there are no answers.

Angels. Angels are what many people turn to and this is what was given to Laurie in one form of healing. An angel to watch over her and her family rested in her living room, hanging from branches of trees. Garrett's angel is watching over Laurie and Tom and Chantal and Kailee as they prepare this book for others to grieve, grow and hope to inspire another young person to stray from this permanent decision.

Bless You Savoie Family for your courageous and creative endeavor.

Diana Flanery

Laurie:

I came across this picture when I was unpacking today. It was taken when I came to Arizona after Chantal was born. I apologize for not being in touch much... time goes by so fast these days.

I intended to contribute to the book you are all doing and I realize the deadline has passed, but wanted to share with you my thoughts.

When your friends called me to tell me of some sad news and shared what had happened in your family, I immediately felt the shock and disbelief. How could this happen? The last time I saw Garrett was when you all visited Niagara and we spent time together at the Marriott. I remembered him swimming in the pool, joking around and watching the fireworks from the room. I thought of the talk we had at the pool; how you were worried about him and some of the challenges he was facing and how you were hoping that in time he would be more settled.

Working as a nurse in mental health, I meet people who have been touched by suicide. I meet people who have tried to hurt themselves or have had family members attempt suicide and succeed. I see the pain that they feel and how they come to live with it every day and work to heal themselves and their families. As I watched Garrett's memorial service, I saw the love that friends and family poured out to all of you and I knew that you would be surrounded by healing power. The "Why?" question is not easy to answer as often there really is no answer. We ask ourselves: Why do bad things happen to good people? Why did this happen to me/us? Trying to answer questions that only God has the answer to will only keep us awake at night--they won't ever be truly answered in this world. We only know that with God's love we have the strength to carry on when bad things happen and trust that He will surround us with the tools we need to heal, to get up the next day and make a difference in the world. You are all truly amazing to share your story with others.

Ann

Dear Laurie,

Good luck with your book. You are doing a wonderful thing. Love you my dear friend!

Joan

I didn't know Garrett personally. He was the son of my friends Laurie and Tom. He was the brother of Kailee and Chantal. I helped Laurie decorate his room in camouflage when he was a young boy. I remember Laurie telling me he wanted to go into the armed services, I think it was flying. I attended his graduation party. He seemed like a happy young man celebrating with all his family and friends. He had plans for his future! What happened?

I was going to breakfast with my daughter, Lauren, when I received that horrible phone call. I can remember it like yesterday. Laurie's friend called to give me the horrific news. I asked if he had been in a car accident. Obviously her response was no. Then I asked if he had killed himself. I don't know why I asked that next, but I did. The world stopped for a few minutes. Why would a young boy in the prime of his life do something like this? There is no answer!

I made some phone calls to inform friends of this horrible news. I needed to do something but what? I brought them food. I hope I brought them some form of comfort by just being there for them. Of course, it was nowhere near enough. I felt so helpless!

I can't begin to imagine the pain Laurie and Tom are going through as parents. I wish I could understand why a child or any human being for that matter would take his own life. I know there is no answer. So many time you will hear, "They were in so much pain they just couldn't handle it anymore". My mother, who was diagnosed with Multiple Sclerosis at the age of 17, was in pain every single day of her life. At the age of 77 she died. I know she would have given anything to live just one more month, one more week, even one more day to see her new great grandson be born. I miss her terribly!

I hope that anyone who is thinking about suicide thinks again. DON'T BE SO SELFISH! There are so many people who love you even when you think there aren't. There are so many people out there who are willing to help you through horrible times. The effects of suicide are everlasting with a rippling effect. There are no do-overs. WHEN YOU ARE GONE YOU ARE GONE FOREVER! I am sure for Laurie, Tom, Kailee and Chantal the pain starts every morning when they rise and never goes away.

I hope this book helps Laurie. More importantly, if this book helps just one person change their mind about suicide then she has accomplished her mission. My heart goes out to the entire Savoie family. If anything I have said is hurtful to them I apologize. They have had too much pain in their lives already. I hope this book will bring them some sort of peace and comfort. They all deserve it!

Joan Saftchick

Hi Laurie,

I'm so sorry I have not sat myself down long enough to put my thoughts together for this very emotional issue.

I have so much I want to put down in words, but I don't want the message to get lost in the history of how our lives came to pass. But at the same time.... If it wasn't for the history of how we became friends I would not have gotten to know Garrett the way I do......without ever getting the chance to meet him while he was on this earth.

But I have met Garrett since his passing more than once and I must say, I'm not sure how to put it into words how he has affected not so much my life, but how I have seen him affect you and your family's life since his passing.

I know this must be difficult and cathartic for you at the same time......I pray I can help bring you peace in what ever words I offer to this project.

Love,

Your friend for life!

Sheryl Rangel-Gethner

Section 7: **FAMILY & FRIENDS: Personal Experiences**

Garrett's suicide, like so many others, stirs memories of others that have been lost by the same tragic circumstances. In this section, family and friends discuss how suicide has touched them in more ways than one. Suicide is a real threat in society and the submissions here indicate how so many people have known several others who have left this world in the same way. Unfortunately, suicide is very far-reaching.

I have written this and erased it more times that I would like to admit which is pretty ironic because I am a writer—words always come easily to me. However, this particular subject leaves me at a loss for words more times than not. It's difficult for me to explain how suicide has impacted my life because honestly so many emotions scream through my mind.

I didn't know Garrett. I am not close to the family. I never knew about his story or the pain that his suicide caused so many of you until I responded to an ad looking for an editor for this book. I was just looking for work, but what I found was a piece of my heart that has been missing for too long.

I was five years old when my father put a bullet in his brain. You would think that a five-year-old would have their age to shield them from such things, but not me. I remember that night so vividly and I know that the details will be with me for a lifetime. I remember the sounds, the smells, hell—I even remember that my nails were dirty as I stared at my hands while my dad did what he thought he needed to.

I remember that my mother was sitting on the edge of the bed in a t-shirt with children's handprints all over it. It said "World's Best Mom". Her hair was down and tangled. She was crying. My dad was slumped in the corner slurring words that I couldn't decipher. He had a gun in his hands. When I moved closer to him, he reached out to me and awkwardly spread a drug-induced smile across his face. I heard him say, "If you have anything to say to me, you better say it now."

I just sat there. I didn't know what to say. What do you say? The truth was that this wasn't the first time my dad had said things like this. I assumed that he would pass out and in the morning it would be as if nothing had happened. That was my normal. That night, he wasn't just high. That night, he had a plan to follow through. My dad managed to drag his addicted body to our front lawn before he pulled the trigger. The quick snap of the gunshot will be a sound I will never forget.

Because I was so young, I have gone through a wide spectrum of emotions about my father's suicide. I remember my first thought about it was that it wasn't real. People don't really die. I remember swinging on my swing set asking the man in the moon to send my daddy back because my mommy cried too much. I didn't understand the finality of death.

As I grew into a pre-teen, I felt anger—lots of anger. I hated him so much for making me "that kid". I hated the way that people would look at me when they realized that my dad was not only dead, but that he did it himself. I must have been a real shit head for him to not want to be around. I had therapy with a bunch of other kids whose dads had died. The idea was good I guess, but all the other kid's dads died from normal things—heart attack, cancer; one kid's dad was a cop that got shot in the line of duty. My dad died because he wanted to. What a bastard.

When I got into my later teens I was able to let go of some of the bitterness. My sister had a really difficult time during our teen years and I focused more on helping her cope with everything. It was really a cop out I think. I compartmentalized my feelings in the name of helping other people. The truth was, I was sick of trying to make sense of a senseless act. It happened and there wasn't a damn thing I could do about it.

Now, I am in my mid-twenties. I have a child. I'm married. I graduated college and I am now obtaining a Master's Degree. There isn't a day that goes by that somewhere in my mind I don't think to myself, *He missed this. All of this.* And for that—I just feel sorry for him.

Life goes on, right?

When I started this project, I was focused on being my typical un-emotional self. I was here to place appropriate commas, edit typos and fill in the blanks. As I read more and more, my wall started to crumble. Suicide hurts and it's okay to not be okay.

While I didn't know Garrett, I think he reminded me of something. Suicide hurts. It hurts a lot. It doesn't matter the relationship that you had with the person, how much time has passed, or how rational you think you should be. Sometimes, you need to scream and cry and be completely—not okay. Maybe that's what people need in order to really heal. Maybe that's what I needed. Laurie, you may ask yourself if this book will help a single person—it already has.

Thanks for letting me be a part of this.

Sheree McDonald - Editor of *the Ripple Effect*

When I think of suicide, I imagine a ripple effect because that's what the suicides in my life have felt like to me. When my friend Ellen died, she believed that it didn't matter whether she was here anymore. Her husband was leaving her for another woman, the company she'd devoted her life to for almost 20 years swept her under the rug like so much garbage, and she had no children to anchor her to this life. I can't imagine the pain she must have been feeling to take her own life but I believe that she would have been amazed and dismayed at the long reaching effects that her death had on her coworkers and friends. My husband John's mother committed suicide when he was in his early twenties. Her death eventually contributed to the murder of her 19 year old daughter. It's only been within the past few years that John's been able to let go of the crippling guilt he felt over his sister's death, and her passing still colors his relationship with his own two daughters.

Sometimes good things like this book can occur because of a suicide, and the good that ripples outward to people who may be suffering terribly will hopefully be felt for years to come. I'm so happy that you are doing this in Garrett's memory and for your family's healing process. I applaud your courage and though I can't pretend to know how it feels to lose a child this way, I truly believe that Garrett is still with you and within you and will be so forever. I love you Laurie!

Laura Lakey

The first encounter I had with the Savoie family was right before G-man decided to end his life. My daughter, Jessica, is sort of a mentor/ friend with their daughter, Chantal. I didn't really know any of the family before his death.

Jessica came home quite concerned for Chantal. We asked her what had happened and she told us. It was such a tragedy to hear this. Chantal really needed a friend to be able to talk to who was outside of the family. Jess was there for her. Talking about things with Jessica helped to release some of the feelings she was having. I believe that God provided Chantal with an ear that really understood what she was going through.

Jessica came to me to tell me that maybe I should talk to Laurie because I would be able to help her through her grief. I had lost my son five years before to a car accident. He was 25 years old. I called Laurie and talked to her hoping that I could be some sort of outside person that she could say anything she felt to without being judged. She opened up immediately as if we had known each other for years. It was a little strange feeling, but we both knew there was a bond. I shared with her and answered her questions. Both of us were blessed. When I went to her house for the celebration of Garrett's life, I didn't know anyone but a few people. It was ok because I knew I needed to be there for her. I could see that this family was hurting at the same time as they were celebrating and could totally relate to their pain.

My belief is that The Lord places people in our lives at just the right time and place. He is faithful to provide every want and need that we have. I also believe that there is nothing that God isn't in control of, especially our time to die. Grief is ok as long as we know that God's will is perfect and that we don't have to like it, but we just need to trust him that he knows exactly what he is doing. I thank God for the Savoies. They have given me strength also and we have made new friends on top of all of it. ☺

With Love,

Debbie Thompson

Hi Laurie,

I did not know Garrett personally, but I have known you for quite some time. I was probably the last to hear about Garrett. I came in for my shift and someone asked me if I would like to sign a card for you, that there had been a death in your family. When I found out it was your son, my heart just stood still. I couldn't help thinking that this could have been my son. I couldn't stop thinking about this for a long time. I still do occasionally.

I can only imagine what this loss must be like for you and your family. I think I have told you that I worry about my son every day. My son has always been extremely emotional, a little wild (just like his mother!), unbelievably talented and very loving. But, with this comes a dark side. I believe this is what causes me to worry and I probably will forever. Everyone tells me to "cut the strings" and just let him live his life, but I will always be watching over him, wondering if there is more I can do for him!

I know I raised my son the best I knew how, making every effort to make sure he was loved, happy and well adjusted. We can only do our best and hope for the best, but unfortunately, we can never predict what the outcome will be.

I hope this is helpful to you in some way!

Best regards,

Linda Martin

As far back as my freshman year of high school, maybe even middle school, suicide has been a part of my life. Two close family friends, not much older than I was at the time, took their lives. One of them was hurting so badly that he took the life of his girlfriend as well. I was heartbroken for these young men, their families, and all of us left without many answers, and more importantly, left without *them*. In fact, I still am. There isn't a week that goes by that I still don't think about them. I can't fathom the loneliness and despair they must have felt then and it was even tougher to understand as a teenager.

Today, as I write this, November 12, 2013, is the eleventh anniversary of my own dad's suicide. The last time I spoke to him was Veteran's Day 2002 when I remember he told me how proud he was of who I was becoming. If I had known that those would be the last words we ever spoke to each other, there is so much more I would have expressed. Unfortunately, because of the way life works, we are not gifted with that opportunity.

A year after 9/11 and after accepting 2 ½ years severance from the only company he'd ever worked for and known, my dad hung himself in his basement, leaving behind my brother, my half-sister and half-brother, my step-mom, and myself. I received my "portion" of the note he left and still to this day, have never seen the other parts of that letter. Needless to say, my heart bears an open wound that only ever partially heals.

I'm 37 years old now. I am a passionate middle school teacher and a loving mom of two of the most awesome kiddos on this planet. I have experienced the heartache of divorce, but I have mended my heart on my own and I am living in the here and now. Unfortunately, my dad has missed it all...the good, the bad, and the life-changing. He left me only knowing me as a brand new teacher trying to figure out life after college. Not the "me" that I would have liked him to have known in the end.

My dad's suicide, along with those of my two childhood friends, was just the beginning of my experiences with this kind of loss. In my lifetime, I have attended the funerals of ten amazing individuals who, unfortunately, didn't have the capacity to realize their importance in this world. I think about each and every one of them often and at different times for different reasons. Their memories are not lost, as I think of them all often.

While my heart has mended itself from various life-changing events, I'm not quite sure that the wounds left from these events will ever be healed. To be honest with you, I'm okay with that fact. It means that I'm *alive!* I can feel hurt and pain and joy and excitement. I'm coping with life's curve balls and ups and downs. And at the same time, I'm making a conscious choice to enjoy all life has to offer.

In the end, I can only hope that all of us seek to be *alive* and to know that it's okay to hurt, to feel lost, or be unsure of the future--every single one of us has experienced these feelings. Seek HOPE...there's hope in even the smallest things around us and to attempt to find them shows how courageous God made us.

"Sometimes even to live is an act of courage."

— Lucius Annaeus Seneca

Shannon Griffith

September 21, 2013

Dear Garrett,

You never really knew me, but as we come upon another anniversary of your death, I want to write you a letter that your family can include in a book they are writing about suicide and how it affects so many lives; even those who never really knew the person who took his/ her own life. So I thought I would just sit down and put down some thoughts about how your death affected myself and our family.

Garrett, I first met your mom through our neighborhood moms group. You and your family used to live in the neighborhood that I moved into 11 years ago. As a matter of fact, we looked at the house your family was selling at the time. When I met your mom and found out you all used to live in this neighborhood and that your house was one of the homes we looked at for sale, I remembered something about your house in particular that I mentioned to your mom. While we were looking at houses to buy, I always paid particular attention to how the current homeowners decorated the home so I could try and visualize what it could look like if we moved into it. And I remember that I had mentioned to our realtor that your house struck me as a very warm, loving place because of all the wonderful family photos all over the various rooms. You all were smiling and looked so happy in the pictures and I could tell what a close-knit family you all were. I know that pictures can often be deceiving, but knowing your family as I do now, I know that was not the case. You all are a close-knit bunch and would do anything for each other. So it really hit me when I found out that you had killed yourself. How could a child with that much love in his family not see that his family would be there for him no matter what he was going through? And that is when I totally realized how SELFISH suicide is!! Having suffered through depression myself, I know how difficult it can be to shake off desperate feelings. But when you give in to that despair and decide not to let someone else help you, you do not realize how much you are robbing someone else of the opportunity to help you and you do not realize what feelings are left behind for those who know and love you to deal with-- not just for a day or two, but for the rest of our lives.

Like I said, Garrett, you and I never met. I saw you a few times when I was at your home with your mom, but we were never officially introduced. But, your mom is one of my closest friends here in Arizona. To watch what she and your dad and your sisters went through, and are still going through, has just been devastating. I see a constant sadness in your family that was never there before and that will never completely go away. I am sure there is not a day that goes by that your family does not think about and grieve for you.

Your mom is laughing again, but it is not the same and probably never will be. A part of all of them died that day with you. I wish you could have seen before all of this how much you were totally loved, not just by your family, but also by so many friends and relatives. Your memorial service was amazing! There were people of all ages, sharing wonderful stories of how much you had touched them. People, who would have wanted to help had they known how much you were hurting.

Garrett, my nephew lost a friend to suicide too. I asked his mom why she thought that boy would take his own life when he had so many people around him that cared for him. She said she knew that his despair had gotten so deep that he couldn't even focus from one minute to the next, much less think about the future for those around him. So I think I can empathize with what you must have been feeling, too. But I so wish you would have asked someone for help and I wish that you could have realized that your family would have been there for you, NO MATTER WHAT! But maybe this book, and all these stories will help someone else. If that is the case then we will all know that your death was not in vain and we can rest just a little knowing that you are still living in spirit with so many others and that you are finally resting in the presence of our awesome God from whom all life is given. Thank you, Garrett, for touching so many people around you. You will never be forgotten and we will never forget!

With thankfulness for your life and for the lessons you are teaching each one of us,

Carrie, Dale, Amy and Erin Almond

November 17, 2010 - The reason I remember the day your son passed away is because it was a very significant day for me as well. I was flying home to New Jersey that day to see my Dad. I had made the decision to go home just that Monday. We had found out on Sunday that my dad had a massive tumor in his chest that was pressing on his esophagus, lungs and heart. He refused any kind of treatment and asked to be checked out of the hospital immediately. He said "I've had a good life, I want to go home." They couldn't give us any idea on how long he had. They said it could be weeks or it could be months. My niece and cousins were scheduled to come out to Arizona the following week for Thanksgiving, so I was torn about whether I should go now or wait until after Thanksgiving. Going now would mean canceling Thanksgiving. A friend at work encouraged me to go now because we could have quality time together while he was still aware. So I was flying home on Wednesday morning. On top of all of this, I received an email from the president of the company that I worked for announcing that our company had been bought out that day. This would mean that I would soon be out of a job.

Because I wasn't going into work that day, I had the pleasure of bringing my kids to school before I left for the airport. I dropped Rebecca off at Sonoran Trails. When I brought Derek to Desert Willow, I parked the car so I could go into the office and talk to Trish for a bit. Laurie was cheerfully manning the student drop-off site. So as I walked Derek onto the school grounds, I stopped to chat with her. We spoke about my situation and she offered me comfort and prayers. She always has kind and encouraging words for me every time I see her! She is the kind of person who builds you up. So I was very grateful to have had the chance to talk with her that day.

The next day, while I was visiting with my dad in New Jersey, I got a call from Colleen Davis and she let me know that your son had taken his life on Wednesday. I felt shock, disbelief and great sadness for you and your family. I always think back on this because, on what would turn out to be one of the most heart-wrenching and tragic days of your life, you were able to give me hope and encouragement in my situation.

My dad passed away that Saturday. I know the sadness and loss that was in my heart that day and how much it hurt. I couldn't begin to imagine what you must have been feeling for the loss of your child, especially under the circumstances. I was so grateful to have been able to sit and talk with my dad before he passed away. It made me really think about how many times we don't get that opportunity to tell the ones we love just how much we love them, how important they are to us, and how our life would be affected if they were not part of it. We never know what life holds for us, so don't ever miss this opportunity! It could change their life and all those around them.

Eva Colombo

I would also like to share a poem by W.H Auden that really moved me:

Funeral Blues – W.H. Auden

Stop all the clocks, cut off the telephone,
Prevent the dog from barking with a juicy bone,
Silence the pianos and with muffled drum
Bring out the coffin, let the mourners come.

Let aeroplanes circle moaning overhead
Scribbling on the sky the message He Is Dead,
Put crêpe bows round the white necks of the public doves,
Let the traffic policemen wear black cotton gloves.

He was my North, my South, my East and West,
My working week and my Sunday rest,
My noon, my midnight, my talk, my song;
I thought that love would last forever: I was wrong.

The stars are not wanted now: put out every one;
Pack up the moon and dismantle the sun;
Pour away the ocean and sweep up the wood.
For nothing now can ever come to any good.

When I learned of Garrett's death, it brought back all that pain I felt when my nephew, Michael, died. Suicide, no matter what the circumstances, is heart-wrenching. To lose a family member, your son, my nephew, anyone, turns the world upside down. How do you go on? It's devastating.

I can't imagine you and your beautiful family going through what my family went through. Why? What more could I have done to help my loved one? That's one of the questions we all seem to ask. I could have called him more often. How could this happen? It's the worst nightmare and you think, *it can't be true, there must be a mistake.* I tried to be strong for my brother and sister-in-law and we would end up crying together. And I still do cry to this day and wish it was a bad dream.

There is nothing more devastating, nothing worse, than losing someone to suicide. We blame ourselves, at least I did. How could I have prevented this? How could I have shown him more of what a great guy he was? So funny, so sweet, so much going for him. How can I now lessen the pain I feel and my family feels every single day? I don't think we, the people who loved that person, can ever be the same.

In the beginning, I just wanted to die too. Then I would be the one hurting my family and friends. I know he didn't plan to hurt anyone, but it does hurt all of us. I couldn't take my life and hurt my family all over again, but then I would be out of my pain. After my experience with my nephew's death, I know that suicide is not an option no matter how unbearable the pain. It's a permanent solution to a temporary problem.

So, we keep putting one foot in front of the other, we stay close with family making sure they know how important they are and how much we love them.

For me, the pain never really has gone away. My life is never going to be the same. All I can do now is try and let everyone I know and love how much they mean to me, how important they are in my life.

I didn't know Garrett and yet, I feel your family's pain and am so sad that someone else I know and love has gone through the same pain and agony that I did and all of my family did.

Maybe I should become a speaker and go to the junior high and high schools. Maybe I must resolve to always let people know how important they are to me. One thing I do know is that I always think about my nephew and how old he would be today--what he would be doing, how he would look as a 23-year- old. Would he be married, have kids, still be in college? I'll never know. All I can do is thank God that I was blessed to have him in my life for 19 years. And how I will never, ever stop thinking about him and wishing he was still here.

I am sorry your family went through this and I wish I could take your pain away. All I can do is be there to listen. To remind people how important they are, how special they are. That the problem is temporary but suicide is forever.

Don't do it. Whoever contemplates suicide please, please, just don't do it. We love you no matter what. Let us help you get through this. It will get better. Know that people love you and if you take your life, your family, your friends and anyone who know you will never truly get over the loss of your life. You are important in the world, please believe that. There is help. Let us help. Talk about it. It helps. Believe me, I know. Just don't do it, please.

We are all special, remember that.

Kim Dudley

Michael and Kim

Hi Laurie,

Attached is the *Fixing It* piece that my husband wrote a while ago and said you could use. Hopefully, your book is going well. Hugh and I pray you can find some peace in the middle of it all. Grief is hard work. Outreach is hard work and yet we share with you a desire to help others going through this as well. Just remember to take time for the two of you, too, individually and as a couple.

Karen (Kim's sister-in-law)

Fixing It

Like many guys, I am a fixer. While not the handyman type, I do my best to fix things around the house be it plumbing, painting, basic electrical or other general stuff. I guess I know just enough to be dangerous. Being a fixer also crosses over into my relationships with others. When my wife, Karen, has a problem I'm quick to provide an answer. However, I've come to realize after 33 years of marriage that in many instances Karen does not want me to fix her problems. She just wants to be heard, to explain the situation and to have me listen to what she is saying. I find this is true of others as well. It's taken me a long time to truly understand this. There have also been cases where I have tried to fix relationships and frankly just made it worse. I guess I've learned the hard way just to listen and not offer advice unless I'm asked for it.

When my son, Michael, became depressed at the age of 18, I was quick to offer advice. I have suffered from depression and anxiety in the past and was sure I knew the right answers. I remember being in the basement with Michael when he was having a difficult day and telling him to trust me; that everything was going to be alright and that I was going to make sure he got better. I was going to fix it. Six months later Michael died. Michael took his own life while I was on a business trip. I failed Michael. I promised that I would take care of things and I didn't. That was almost three years ago (April 1, 2009) and there isn't an hour that goes by that I don't think of him. I used to sit inside Michael's closet and pull his clothes down on top of me and just cry. I smelled his scent and that comforted me. But, after a few months the scent was gone and the pain seemed to get worse. I used to go on business trips every other week and sit in my hotel room at night and just scream into the pillow. I remember it feeling so surreal. This can't be happening! It's got to be a bad dream! Michael was always so happy and had a smile that lit up the room. He loved making people laugh. He was a goofball and at 6'7" tall was impossible to miss. He was an excellent student and never had any problems with drugs or alcohol. How can this be? And where was God in all of this? I began to question God. Where were you? Why didn't you stop him?

As time went on, I began filling my time with work as much as possible. When not at work, I would read books or play a game on my cell phone. Anything I could do to not talk about it and not face my failure as a father. I also began drinking. One or two glasses of wine a night were just enough for me to get tired enough and I would end up just going to bed. At times, it got to three or four glasses a night. Rationally, I knew that I did my best but in my heart I felt that I failed Michael and that I could never make it up to him or my family. I remember after Michael died that Karen dove into a lot of volunteer organizations, support groups and even training on how to identify "at risk" youth and what to do if you thought they were suicidal. Not me. Sure, I would go to a support group every couple of weeks but after 20-30 minutes I felt the room was closing in on me and I had to escape. As a husband to Karen and a father to Ryan, my oldest son, I was pretty useless, and the drinking was making it worse. Self- medicating was making it worse. I had failed Michael and now I was failing Karen and Ryan, too. Sure, I provided for the family financially, but I wasn't really there for them emotionally, where they really needed me. I saw their pain and I felt like more of a failure. I wanted to fix it for them and I wanted to make them happy again. Every time I saw Karen cry, which was every day, I felt more like a failure. What kind of father was I that my son would take his own life? What kind of man am I when I can't make things better for my wife and eldest son? I wanted to make them happy again and I wanted to take away their pain. I tried to be there for Karen and Ryan emotionally, but my need to escape would kick in and I didn't listen well.

I started seeing a counselor and I think I have made some very positive steps. I'm beginning to realize that trying to fix things for my family is not what's best for me and it's not what's best for them, either. I'm learning that before I can help them I first have to help myself. I was useless to everyone until I started getting myself on the road to recovery. I'm learning that each of us has to grieve in our own way and in our own time. For some, it is through talking about it, some journaling, some art, etc. Some, like me, try to bury it and keep ourselves busy with other tasks, but after a while it becomes very apparent that burying it doesn't work. And neither does self-medicating. I needed to talk about my intense feelings of pain and grief as well as my feelings of failure as a father and a husband. I'm learning that grieving is part of the healing process.

I'm starting to believe that I am not a failure, neither as a father nor as a husband. I did my very best with Michael and I loved him with all my heart. I still do and I always will. I know Michael knows that as he looks down on me today from heaven. I will also continue to do my very best to be a good husband to Karen and father to Ryan. I'm learning to listen well and be there for them whenever they need to talk or give them space when talking isn't what they need. I will continue to do my very best and I will trust God that what happens is His plan. I still make a lot of mistakes and at times try to fix things for Karen and Ryan, but more often than not, I just try to listen and to be there for them. I still miss

Michael so much and I know I always will, but I know that I will be with Michael again in heaven. I look forward to the day when I can hold him again and tell him how much I love him. Until then, I will be the best husband to Karen, father to Ryan and grandfather to my granddaughter, Elle. She never got to know her Uncle Michael but I will make sure that she knows him intimately as she grows up.

Lastly, I've come to accept that we don't always understand God's big plan. I believe God has a plan for all of us. I don't believe He in any way caused Michael's death, but he has used it for good. Through Karen's and my efforts in working with suicide prevention organizations we have been able to help others. We have even had some teenagers and young adults tell us that they were considering suicide, even had a plan in some cases, but are on the road to recovery now. I know this is from God, not because of Karen or me. I still ask God, *Why? Why didn't you stop Michael? And why didn't you answer our prayers when we prayed for you to help Michael?* I even remember Michael saying that he had prayed often to God to take the sadness away. He didn't understand why God wasn't listening. I now understand that God always answers prayer, it just isn't always the way we want Him to. I realize now that God was with Michael the whole time. He held him close when he died and He is with Michael now in paradise. He has also held my family and I close over the past three years. We wouldn't have made it through this terrible time without God carrying us through. I truly don't know how anyone gets through the death of a loved one without faith in our Lord Jesus. I don't understand why Michael died and I probably never will. At least not until I am with him in heaven, but I know God is with Karen, Ryan, Elle and I as we walk move forward in life. His hand is always there for us to grasp and He never leaves our side. We just need to trust Him and hold on tight.

Hugh Hudson

You never know how you will influence or touch someone in life. It might be one word, phrase or an action that influences us on life's pathway. I believe that Garrett's choice will influence so many people in a positive way that the full effect will never be known. Truly, making one person think twice before making such a permanent and devastating decision is profound.

I had a high school friend who, at age nineteen, made the decision to take his life. Over the past 29 years I have thought of him often. I'm sure his choice has affected my attitude towards life, my relationships and decisions I've made. I am sure that Garrett will live on in the consciousness of his loved ones in the same way.

Elaine Bishop

Dear 15 year old me,

You are feeling lost right now, like there is no way out. You don't fit in, people are being mean, and all you want is to be appreciated for who you are. I want to say that I do, I appreciate you for who you are. And I love who you are. And here is why.

You become me. The feelings of insecurity, depression and confusion turn into confidence, happiness and passion. The pain you feel right now will make you stronger in the end. They have made me stronger.

It hasn't been an easy road to become me. I have had more experiences with insecurity, bullying and feeling that there is no way out. I wish I could tell you that those feelings and experiences stayed in high school, but they didn't. There will always be cruel people in this world who will put you down because you aren't like them. That is their problem and the only feeling they deserve from you is pity. You can't let them keep you down.

It gets better. It gets A LOT better. It becomes incredible. You will find that thirst for life that makes you want to keep living, and living fiercely. I have found that thirst, and in it I have found myself, so know that you will.

Life is not easy. Obstacles will be thrown at you from all angles, but there comes a time where you will be able to push them out of your way, ignore the naysayers, and prove everyone wrong. And more importantly, you will prove to yourself that you can overcome everything. And you will, because I have.

There is a light at the end of the tunnel. I am here. You will get here with a smile on your face. Trust and believe in yourself and beautiful things will happen. There is so much love to find in this world, in every shape and form. Continue being you, because if you hadn't kept being you, I wouldn't be me.

And "me" is pretty amazing.

Love,

23 year old you

Gill

Laurie,

When I received the call about my friend who had taken his life, I was in complete shock. I had just read his Facebook posts and he seemed so happy with life. It was overwhelming to think he was really gone. I remember looking at his name in my phone and thinking if I just called he would answer. A few nights after this event I had a dream. I woke up to my friend in my room. I asked him what he was doing here and if he was okay. He told me he had gone to sleep and wasn't going to be waking up this time. We talked for a while and I was reassured he was happy and okay. When he could fly out of my room I knew he was in a better place and it brought me the peace I needed.

Anytime I think about my friend, I wish I could have reached out to him. "If only I had known" is what we all say to ourselves, but no one can truly understand what another is going through and make their decisions for them. Each person who knew him misses him and loves him dearly. We all can reminisce about the great moments we had with him and have the faith that he is now in a place of peace and love.

Amberley Schneider

POETRY

Many people find it easier to express themselves through an artistic avenue. The following entries are pieces of poetry that loved ones wanted to share about their feelings of Garrett and suicide overall.

Choose to Live

Life is a gift so precious and rare.
It can be hard sometimes and Difficult to bear.

Please remember this life is a series of tests
Take one day at a time and do your very best.

You were born into a family to help as a guide.
Tell them of your feeling, please don't keep them hidden inside.

It is sometimes hard to see beyond this very day.
Please trust in God, he will show you the way.

Life has more to offer than this moment of pain.
At times it is hard to dance in the rain.

The Storm will pass, it is not too long... just hang on.
You have no idea what is lost, if you are gone.

Just up ahead and just down the road.
If you walk by faith you are never alone.

Great times, laughing and smiles are up ahead.
Stop focusing on now and wishing to be dead.

You must see that there is a bigger picture, in all there is to do.
Remember you are precious and no one wants to be without you.

By: Mary Porter

Dedicated
To all those that are hurting.
I love you and God does too.

Garrett, Where Have You Gone? By Mary Hahn

We lost so early your shining light!
From this world of pain and hope
The numbness, we feel is hauntingly real
How are we to cope?

You taught us so much in your short time
Today, you are still teaching us life's hard choices
Daily, we feel you working with our precious children lost
Playing, helping and teaching them and we rejoice!

Your gifts that you shared with others on earth
Are still being shared and developed above?
The small children look up to you
And grow daily in their love.

You inspire, encourage and love gently
Showing us the way from darkness into light
Garrett, you are with us daily
Our pain has turned to hope as we soar to new heights.

We love you and you are greatly missed
Your pain is gone and now your light shines through
Ever brighter like a twinkling star
In everything you do and in us too!

Laurie, below is a 'musing' that I'm honored to share with you as I think of the spirit who came in the form of your son. I wanted to hold onto it and finesse it forever and then decided to send it to you as is. I trust you will receive it feeling the intent of love with which it is offered.

Take care of yourself. With Blessings.

<u>But For the Grace of God</u>

As spirit, so temporary in human form,

This game we play – the hide and seek –

Seems so real!

For many of us, so young

We forget who we really are.

Forgotten through the years.

And the pain of our earth stories,
Seems so real, making us feel so alone.

In these storied moments we at times believe,

The best decision is to go back;

Back from where we came,

To where we all return

Releasing this form.

And so.......

Some 'rush back' to be who we are.

Some 'stay' to be who we are,

All remembering, seeing a glimpse.......

Aaah - then ultimately knowing:

We do not come or go.

We exist as we always are,

With or without physical form.

As one universal consciousness,

Never alone.

Those who choose to drop this form,

Those who choose to keep this form,

Are but one,

Safe in that oneness;

Exercising free will within universal love.

However we manifest that consciousness,

It does not end, ever,

But will be continued forever,

Together, as one,

And never alone.

Kiki Hobin

Hi Laurie,

When someone leaves this world by their choice,

We only wish they could have heard our voice.

It leaves a dark and aching hole in our heart.

Now that they're gone, we will fall apart.

If you know someone going down this road,

Please let them know they are not alone.

For when they're gone, there's a void to fill,

They don't really know how this makes us feel.

Family, friends and even strangers are there,

To guide and love and show that they care.

Love, Dana Kazemi ~ Arizona 2013

Photo by Barbara - Hand Reaching Down from Heaven

Missing You

Death is inevitable
It is what makes us human.
No matter what we do with our life
We know that ultimately we leave the ones we love
the ones we cherish,
the ones that make us who we are.

Death is inevitable
It is the common core of our understanding.
Yet the loss of a loved one gone too soon is paralyzing.
The heartache is immense, the questions are overwhelming,
the emptiness is utterly daunting.
Missing You

Barbara Hernández

Open Love Letter to Child . . . Consider for a Moment

Nothing is as powerful as my immense love for You. From the moment I saw You, this is a love like no other. A fierce, lioness love to protect You forever.

Consider for a moment: from Your helpless first days of life, until my last breath, this love endures.

This love knows no bounds, and is not diminished by any word or act. Of all I want for You, my Child – is for my love to keep You safe.

Consider for a Moment:

When something happens to You, it happens ten-fold to me.

When You are happy, I am happy.

When You hurt, I hurt.

When You are sad or troubled, I feel the physical and emotional pain.

If You get cut, I bleed. If You fall, I am bruised.

When You think You do not matter,

Consider for a Moment: the effect on me. No matter what Your age, I feel the impact.

You are the most important part of my life. Everything I do or do not do, is because of You.

Consider for a Moment: how what happens to You, impacts me.

If You do not like yourself, I feel You do not like me.

When You do not love Yourself, I feel You do not love me.

If You do not care, I feel uncared for.

Consider for a Moment: God put You on this Earth.

Consider for a Moment: God makes no mistakes.

Your importance in this World is immense. What You, my Child, at any age, mean to the World is to be You. Perfect, flawed, happy, sad, calm, or troubled, God has a plan.

Consider for a Moment: When the World seems intimidating and daunting; it is only because Your role in it is fully known only to God.

Whether World-known or Home-known, You have made Your mark - in my heart, in my soul. That is no small feat. Your impact on this fierce protector is only the beginning. Your impact on others is yet to come.

Consider for a Moment: Choose Your life. Try it, Live it. Your adventures are yet to come. Whatever Your purpose in life, how great or small, it is to live it to the fullest.

You are here, no matter Your size, mind, body, accomplishments, goals, or fears, for at least one purpose. To be loved.

If You cannot consider Your impact on the World,

Consider for a Moment: the impact on who cherishes You above all else. Let me love You, hold You, touch You - every day.

Consider for a Moment . . .

Love Always and Forever,

Mom

Lisa Gervase

I sat for a long time not knowing what to write…

As I met you *after* Garrett took his Life…

It caused me to think back on all I once knew

Since childhood – all those people who could not make it through…

And often I wondered: "If they stayed one more day…

Would that 'corner' show up, turning things in a new way?"

Not one of us knows what Life brings us to deal

As we Pray for the Strength to continue – and Heal.

What happens after the fact is unkind –

As we toss it and turn it around in the mind.

Those feelings that must have been in there so deep –

To take over one's actions, beyond Love they keep.

And if one hides their pain so another can't know-

Oh my God – There's a Path – No One wants to go…

And if there's a sense that *something's* not flowing-

One can only help where *allowed*, there IS no knowing.

And for those left who look at the possibilities

Of a Life yet to come, Joys and responsibilities…

We place our values – but they don't apply…

No matter how much, we'll never truly know *why*

Or *what* has occurred – or the thoughts in another –

Questions that haunt – for a Father and Mother –

And Sister and Brother – Loved Ones and Friends

Who gather together when a Life comes to End.

There's guilt and there's sadness – and "second-guessing"

And Grief beyond measure… We ask for a Blessing –

Blessing of Soul and of Family –

For all that has happened – Beyond what we could see.

I do know our Creator LOVES Each One and All –

Whether they soar or excel, falter or fall…

Our Father Forgives – 'cause it's ALL ABOUT LOVE –

And your tears, they are recognized from Above…

Garrett's Soul has been cleared so when he tries again –

In another Life – He'll incarnate and then –

He'll overcome All of his challenges too

And you must make Peace with the Best you can do.

Did you show your Love? Well of course, that's a fact

It's not your Love that's faltered – It's still intact.

This was not your doing, nor of family –

The design of another is - all theirs, you see.

I may not know your family, but I know your *heart*, Laurie

And I know Garrett's now sitting among God's Glory!

And Smiling at ALL OF YOU – NOW <u>FEELING</u> the LOVE –

And is Touched by the Caring – from Up Above!

And while not in 3-D, His Spirit is Whole-

And Recognizes your Honor <u>for Him</u>, in this goal.

And in His name, he's part of this Loving Act –

To Inspire others in 'loss' – after the fact!

What a Lesson for All of Us – to see the *Worth*

as One Life Touches So Many Others on Earth!

May this Book of Honor Help ALL of You –

And All Who are Dealing with this Painful Grief too.

Written with much Love, great respect and enormous empathy for all who are affected by Garrett's passing and all who are dealing with the suicide of someone they love.

Andi Feinberg

Hi Laurie – Thanks for the opportunity to contribute to Garrett's book. Here is our submission.

Shout out loudly if you need us

Use your boldest, strongest voice

I didn't hear you, no one heard you, you were silent

Couldn't we together have found a better answer?

I miss your laughter, we miss your spirit

Death cannot be undone

Everyday our heart still bleeds for you

The wisest words were shared by the Savoies in the light of their family tragedy, "Reach out and hug your kids, tell them you love them every day."

The Amy's

Dear Garrett,

We have never met, but your family and your story has touched my life. I wanted to write to you to let you know how much your presence still fills our community and keeps us connected. I found an anonymous poem that really expresses this idea.

Those we love don't go away,

They walk beside us every day,

Unseen, unheard, but always near,

Still loved, still missed and very dear.

Those we love remain with us

For love itself lives on,

And cherished memories never fade

Because a loved one's gone.

Those we love can never be

More than a thought apart,

For as long as there is memory,

They'll live on in the heart.

Garrett, you truly are very much alive in many hearts. Every time I see your mom, I think about the beautiful picture of your family shown on the back of the handout distributed at your service. I think about all the people who were also touched by your "beaming smile" and the joy you radiated with your presence. I think about the stories shared by your loved ones and the tears shed by so many.

I truly believe that you are still filling people with joy, only now there is a pain that accompanies that joy because you are only spiritually present. So many people wish we could experience more time with you, laugh again with you, and make even more memories with you…even people like me who only know you through a family member.

Because of your strong presence with all of us, you are still making a difference. You continue to touch the lives of so many, just like the poem above conveys.

There is one more poem I'd like to share. It is about hope. It can apply to those of us who need help understanding why you're gone. It can apply to those of us still grieving and having trouble living without you. It can apply to those who might also be questioning this life.

For me, every time I see your mom I feel hope. I am uplifted by her strength which I know has a lot to do with you. I hope to meet you in heaven someday. And even though we never met, I'll recognize your "beaming smile" and know you as the one who touched so many here on earth.

With love,

Angie Mullenmeister

(Another Cave Creek mother)

You Still Have Hope

If you can look at the sunset and smile, then you still have hope

If you can find beauty in the colors of a small flower, then you still have hope

If you can find pleasure in the movement of a butterfly, then you still have hope

If the smile of a child can still warm your heart, then you still have hope

If you can see the good in other people, then you still have hope

If the rain breaking on a roof top can still lull you to sleep, then you still have hope

If the sight of a rainbow still makes you stop and stare in wonder, then you still have hope

If the soft fur of a favored pet still feels pleasant under your fingertips, then you still have hope

If you meet new people with a trace of excitement and optimism, then you still have hope

If you give people the benefit of a doubt, then you still have hope

If you still offer your hand in friendship to others that have touched your life, then you still have hope

If receiving an unexpected card or letter still brings a pleasant surprise, then you still have hope

If the suffering of others still fills you with pain and frustration, then you still have hope

If you refuse to let a friendship die, or accept that it must end, then you still have hope

If you look forward to a time or place of quiet and reflection, then you still have hope

If you still buy the ornaments, put up the Christmas tree or cook the supper, then you still have hope

If you can look to the past and smile, then you still have hope

If, when faced with the bad, when told everything is futile, you can still look up and end the conversation with the phrase..."yeah...BUT.," then you still have hope

Hope is such a marvelous thing. It bends, it twists, it sometimes hides, but rarely does it break. It sustains us when nothing else can. It gives us reason to continue and courage to move ahead, when we tell ourselves we'd rather give in

Hope puts a smile on our face

when the heart cannot manage.

Hope puts our feet on the path when our eyes cannot see it

Hope moves us to act

when our souls are confused of the direction.

Hope is a wonderful thing, something to be cherished and nurtured, and something that will refresh us in return.

And it can be found in each of us, and it can bring light into the darkest of places.

Never lose hope!

By: Author unknown

Teach Your Children

Crosby, Stills, Nash and Young

You who are on the road

Must have a code that you can live by

And so become yourself

Because the past is just a good bye.

Teach your children well,

Their father's hell did slowly go by,

And feed them on your dreams

The one they picked, the one you'll know by.

Don't you ever ask them why, if they told you, you would cry,

So just look at them and sigh and know they love you.

And you, of tender years,

Can't know the fears that your elders grew by,

And so please help them with your youth,

They seek the truth before they can die.

Can you hear and do you care and

Can't you see we must be free to

Teach your children what you believe in.

Make a world that we can live in.

Teach your parents well,

Their children's hell will slowly go by,

And feed them on your dreams

The one they picked, the one you'll know by.

Don't you ever ask them why, if they told you, you would cry,

So just look at them and sigh and know they love you.

Submitted by Tracy and Barry Carlson

"Savoie"
Final Mix
B.M.

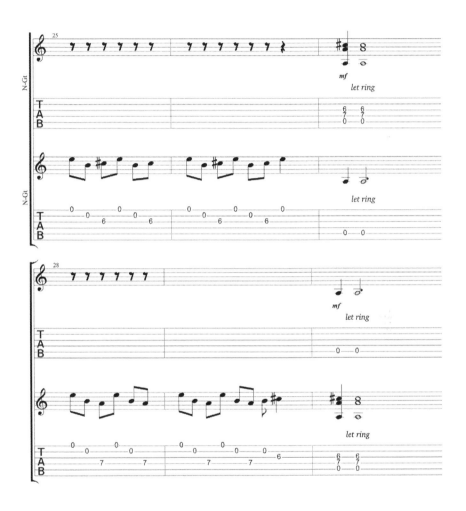

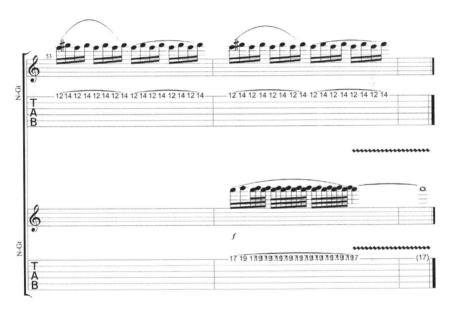

Sheet Music by Benjamin Mach

BEHIND THE BOOK

This book was purposefully written for students in middle school, high school and college, teen groups, churches, SOS groups (Survivors of Suicide), therapist and doctors' offices, and anyone who wants to learn more and/or is concerned about a friend or loved one.

To all of you who contributed to this tapestry of emotions, feelings, support, love, I thank you from the bottom of my heart. I just KNOW we will impact someone, somehow, somewhere for the better.

To all of you who felt that you were not ready to or unable to contribute, *I get it.* This is why I wrote the original letter inviting you to participate the way that I did, open - ended, because this is such a personal thing. (see page 22 for the letter I sent inviting people to participate in the creation of the Ripple Effect.) Everyone has a unique connection and experience to Garrett's death, and everyone is at a different place, comfort, and coping level. *I get it.*

To Garrett's friends who told me, "I just can't articulate how I feel about him, this situation. I can't even begin to put it into words. I can't do it justice. I don't even know how to word my feelings" ... *I get it.* Although participating in the creation of this book may not have been the right timing for you, I still do encourage you to write it out for yourself, anyways. Maybe just getting it out will help your healing as well.

Kailee's addition: If there is one thing I have learned, it's that it is never too late to do something healing for yourself if that is what you need.

To my family, most of whom were not ready to contribute their own passages in here, *I get it.* This is very personal and far too emotional. Trust me, I wish we weren't writing about this.

During the time that I was still collecting everyone's responses who had been invited to participate in the creation of this book, my oldest daughter, Kailee, and I had been having a conversation about whether or not I had given everyone the right amount of time to process, decide if this was a project they would like to be a part of? Kailee said, "Mom, if everyone who would like to contribute is not ready yet, maybe this will be like a Chicken Soup thing, where people will contribute as they can, and we can add it in if we have a second edition?" Who knows?

I still truly believe there isn't anything like this out in the World, yet. Would it have been easier to keep this "safe" in my computer? Yes.

But if our experiences can provide insight to, provide hope for, or bring peace to someone else, even just one person, then it is worth the risk of being completely vulnerable and releasing this out into The Universe rather than keeping it safely on my hard drive. I know these words will get to those who need to hear this message.

I was given the idea to write this book from Divine. Despite having no previous knowledge on how to write or publish a book, it was amazing and interesting to me to see that I trusted that this was what I needed to do, the "right people" were seemingly placed in my path exactly as I needed them to be:

Kim E, who I phoned with this idea, and who immediately saw the need for this book. "Laurie, I could have a whole bookshelf full and just hand them out. I deal with this every day!"

Stephen G, who I met at a dinner party in Canada. He is an author and had just come out with his third book when I reached out to him. He assisted me in getting clear on why I was doing this and gave me lots of hard "homework".

Next Courtney L, who told me she self- published her book and used two websites to find an editor.

Then, using those 2 websites, I had to shut my proposal down because I got 60 requests to edit from all over the World! From North America, Europe, UK, Asia and even India!

It was so apparent that Sheree, my editor, was placed in my path to become the one for this project, which became personal, and healing for her too.

I then met Sandra C, an author of a #1 International bestselling book, We Don't Die, who offered to help me in any way she could, not even knowing what the book was about.

Garrett's friend Jessica L had offered from the beginning to help with graphic design. Well, she not only did that, she motivated me to keep going, when I wanted to keep it "safe" in my computer.

Acknowledgements and Thanks:

Where to begin:

Firstly, God, my Angels, Garrett, and all the other Divine support who first brought me this idea, put up with me arguing for 10 days before I gave in and realized this is pretty powerful and needs to be done.

To my immediate family, Tom, Kailee and Chantal who had to be on board with this, as a family. Even though Tom couldn't write for this, he has been so supportive of the time, energy, sadness, I have been going through to put this together to help others. He has held our family together with his continual love, strength, wisdom, kindness and overall "greatness". I love you all.

To Kim E, my amazing therapist, life coach and book guide, who assisted in choosing an editor and much, much more. In three hours, Kim did what would have taken me three weeks. For all of the support, editing my words, helping with my thoughts, and even supporting this financially.

To Barbara HW, for organizing and sorting all of the entries into the format you now see. More importantly, for the encouragement she gave me as a friend, when she was also in the grieving process for her beloved brother, Freddie.

To Kim D, who helped me interview Sheree for the editor position, and afterwards, in unison, we both said "she's perfect!", for the continual support, love, encouragement she provided daily with such beautiful words, cards, texts, love and support to get this book out to help others!

To Sheree M, for not only being great to work with, you became my cheerleader, and put so much more into the book with your great ideas, and your own amazing contribution.

To my constant supporters: Shirley D and Betsy M, for always encouraging me, throughout this process with your words of strength and love, I'm grateful.

To my proof readers: Kim D, who cried through the first read, and had to reread to make comments. *Barb C*, who cried too, and gave awesome feedback and support "Wow, wow, wow!" *Kiki H*, who said she would be honored and had only minimal changes combined with lots of love and supportive words for me, of why this book was necessary.

To *Liz C* and *Kathleen R*, who wanted to support me not by words but by financial support to ensure this book came to fruition.

To *Jessica L*, for designing this amazing book, for her creative ideas, for tackling this project, in the midst of dealing with the loss of her friend, Garrett. I can honestly and lovingly say, "I wish I had known you when Garrett was alive, but I now have a new, beautiful friend who I adore, admire and love, who will be in my life forever". You have done an AMAZING job with your hours and hours of emotional labor to make this into a beautiful book.

To *April F,* who changed the way I grieved for my beautiful son, by bringing me messages from him from heaven, and continuing to do so.

To *Shari M*, my beloved friend who I told about this idea June 2013 right after I had received the message about it. You wrote for it even before receiving the letter! It amazes me about the "right people", you are like my Sister. You were at the beginning of this book process, and now in June 2014 you have become the "last person" to proof-read the nearly completed manuscript and give me your honest opinion before it goes to publishing.

Also, to ALL, so many Earth Angels, who assisted us right after, and for many, many months later. You will recognize who you are and if I forgot anyone I am truly sorry, I definitely wasn't on the planet after 11-17-10.

Recognizing someone who slept on the floor at the foot of my bed, who made a pot of soup that never seemed to run out, my girlfriends who brought over food and wine right after, my friends who came and had a drink with me to numb the pain, someone who brought their trailer over, two fruit baskets, many, many of you, I think 50 at one time doing yard work, cleaning my house. To all who were part of "Command Central" at the kitchen table, doing tasks, no one wants to even think about. To DWES parents for all of the support, love and meals for many months afterwards. To my friend who still has her purple cleaning gloves here.

To my Bunco girls, who brought over a candle, pajamas for Chantal and an Angel tree and invited the community to come over and fill it. It is so full, and beautiful filled with messages of hope, love and communication! But mostly, love. Again, for coming over the next year on 11-17-11 and bringing a beautiful lit Angel for our backyard.

For all my friends, who kept inviting me to everything even though I basically "hermitized" myself this past year, coping, healing, ...while compiling this book, Thank You for not giving up on me. I love you and appreciate you all.

Hello all who have read some, all, bits of this book, or passed it to someone they knew and cared for, who could benefit from this book:

My HOPE is that this book touches someone ... somewhere ... somehow ... for the better. That you feel, see, appreciate joy, feel love and peace, and if not, Communicate ... ask for help, something Garrett didn't do with us, his family, or friends clearly enough.

I hope that you see from this book what an amazing young man Garrett was (is in spirit). How polite, gentlemanly, and gentle he was. How his great sense of humor could get you laughing. I hope you get a sense of his beautiful smile and eyes, his personality. Although Garrett was shy, once he knew you, he was a loyal friend. He was loving to animals, to people, to life.

One thing that has been made VERY CLEAR to me, is that suicide is not something people want to talk about at all! Many, many people have not contributed to this book, because they can't go there emotionally yet, maybe not ever. Anyway, I know God and many Divine Angels will see that the people who needed to contribute did so, and we may never know how a nugget or word someone has written will affect and help others.

What I would like to leave open-ended out of this book, life, tragic experience ... is for anyone who is touched by this, these stories, who have their own experiences and want to help others (the suckers left behind, as I call us) feel free to send your words to me. Maybe we'll have a 2nd version, who knows?

The more information we can share with the world, the more the people IN the world will know their worth. That is what I WISH Garrett had known in his time on Earth.

With much love and gratitude to all,

Garrett's Mom, Who Loves Him So Very Much, Laurie

The Angel Tree

This Angel Tree is not only a tree,
It is a friendly tree that is always watching over you.

This Angel Tree is not only a tree,
It is a magical tree that makes miracles happen,
hopes become reality and nevers become always!

This Angel Tree is not only a tree,
It is where everything started.

It is the Tree of Life.

Please enjoy our Angel Tree!
Our hope is that this tree will be filled with memories of Garrett
and inspirations for his amazing family!

Please take a look each day to see what the angels have placed in
the tree to bring joy to all of you!

With Love,
Your Bunco Gals

Photograph by Shari Melnychuk

I had the extraordinary privilege of meeting Garrett and subsequently getting to know his lovely family after his passing. Yes, I said *after* his passing.

I am a sensitive and as such on occasion people who have crossed into spirit seek me out to relay messages from them to their living relations.

I did not know or know of the Savoie family prior to this incident, but was good friends with Garrett's Great Auntie Isobel. She at no time mentioned Garrett, his passing or his family.

I was home alone one evening when I suddenly had an overwhelming urge, well prodding really, from spirit to call my friend, Isobel. I always listen to my spirit guide and as such, I called her.

As Isobel and I began to speak, this handsome young man presented in full solid form. I only knew that he was in spirit as he had an auric glow about him.

He went on to tell me his name, about his family and his passing.

He especially wanted to impart to his family and in particular his mother, that his passing was by his hand, he was remorseful that he had hurt those that he had left behind, but was very at peace and happy with his spirit life.

He wanted to let his family know that he works with children in the spirit world, teaching them music and helping them transition. His transition was very easy, and while some people who pass by their own hands have an orientation/counselling time on the other side, Garrett didn't need very much of this and adapted to his new environment very quickly and easily.

Although he did realize that passing in the way he did was not the best choice, it was his time to exit from the physical plane. His work here was done.

It has been my great pleasure to meet Garrett and to be able to help his family with their grieving process, to help them heal and come to terms with his passing into spirit. They know that although he is not with them in physical form, he is and will continue to be with them in spirit form.

I wish loving and healing light to everyone. Know that our loved ones are all okay and living in a fabulous realm.

April Farrall

Hi Laurie,

I've attached low resolution files of the pencil drawing, colored pencil drawing, and a possible suggestion (not the finished cover, just a comp) for the cover for you to think about. If you want to send me an idea of what you want the cover to say, I can incorporate it into the layout. I imagine a ripple effect because that's what the suicides in my sphere have felt like to me.

Love ya,

Laura

P.S. Until I really looked at his photos, I didn't realize what a beautiful boy he was. He had amazing eyes!

Along with my submission letter, I left Laurie a little note offering to help with the book. Laurie didn't want to burden me, but I convinced her that I truly wanted to help. It happened to be the same day she was determined to get the book off the ground. I will tell you this, I would never undo my offer as it has allowed me to do something good and meet a wonderful friend, but it has also been one of the hardest challenges I've had to face.

I am so thankful to have met the Savoies. I admire their strength in turning the worst moment of their life into a powerful tool to help others. Thanks to this book, even more people will grow to love Garrett and he will continue to live on and change lives. I feel this book is extremely powerful and I pray that it will have a positive impact on people.

Love Always,
Jessica Lehr

Hi Laurie,

Here is the message I promised you ...

The Ultimate Gift, by Jim Stovall, is a book I highly recommend for ALL young people to read! It will enlighten them to the wonderful gift of life and the many other gifts God has already given them. Sometimes a young person gets caught up in peer pressure, not fitting in, or comparing themselves to others. If they can step out of that box for a moment to appreciate what they DO have, ie. sight, family, shelter, food, transportation, etc., then sometimes they can focus on helping others and take opportunities that promote giving. Giving of themselves, their time, their knowledge, will take the focus off "self" and help them realize their full potential as a human being. Volunteerism can foster this sense of giving. I recommend it start early and often.

Laurie, don't know if this is what you had in mind for your book, but feel free to use it if it serves a purpose.

Respectfully,
Lynn Clayton

Laurie,

I was thinking that if you don't have a title for the book yet, *The Ripple Effect* might be appropriate. When my good friend, Ellen, killed herself many years ago, I was amazed at the long-reaching influences that her act caused. My husband John's mother committed suicide when he was 23 and we're still feeling the ripples. I don't think that most people, particularly younger people, realize just how connected they are to everyone and indeed to the whole world. Anyway, I gave John a photo of Garrett to draw for me and I'll color it as soon as he's finished. If you think you might like to use the title I suggested, I could send you a file with just the art of Garrett and another with Garrett and waves of ripples extending out from him. Just a thought.

Love,

Laura

Laura Lakey

Freelance Illustrator and Designer

E-Mail: **AZLakey@yahoo.com**

Website: **www.CowgirlPinupArt.com**

Illustration by John Lakey & Laura Lakey

Helping Parents Heal

Helping Parents Heal is a non-profit organization dedicated to assisting parents who have lost children, giving them support and resources to aid in the healing process. We go a step beyond other groups by allowing the open discussion of spiritual experiences and evidence for the afterlife, in a non-dogmatic way. Affiliate groups are expected to welcome everyone regardless of religious (or non-religious) background and allow for open dialog.

Our Facebook page is Parents United in Loss, aka Helping Parents Heal, and our website is **www.HelpingParentsHeal.info**

Co-Founders Contact Info:
Mark Ireland: **Mark@MarkIrelandAuthor.com**
Elizabeth Boisson: **EVBoisson@yahoo.com**

Sheri Perl

www.SheriPerl.com is the home of The Prayer Registry.

The Prayer Registry is for parents who have lost children. Each child registered and their family receives mass prayer every year on the anniversary day of the child's passing. No anniversary goes by that these children and their families are not honored. To register your child for prayer send the full name and passing date to Sheri at: **ThePrayerRegistry@gmail.com.** Everyone is welcome to join. The Prayer Registry is a free service.

April Farrall

Psychic, Intuitive Healer, Angel Communicator

604.727.4399

White Rock B.C., Canada

Jessica Lehr

Graphic Designer, Illustrator

E-Mail: **JessLehrDesigns@gmail.com**

Website: **www.JessicaLehr.com**

The Ripple Effect

If you want to share any stories please send to:

E-Mail: **RippleEffect2010@gmail.com**

or to our website: **www.SuicidesRippleEffect.com**

Kim Evans

Transformational / Success Coach

E-Mail: **Info@Your-Wings.com**

Website: **www.Your-Wings.com**

Hotlines

National Suicide Prevention Lifeline
1.800.273.TALK (8255) - 24/7 Suicide Prevention Lifeline
www.suicidepreventionlifeline.org

EMPACT – Suicide Prevention Center
1.800.SUICIDE & 1.800.656.HOPE - 24/7 Crisis Hotline
www.lafronteraaz.org

GLBT National Help Center
1.888.843.4564
www.glnh.org

GLBT National Youth Talkline
1.800.246.PRIDE (7743)
www.glnh.org

TEEN Lifeline
800.248.TEEN
602.248.TEEN
www.teenlifeline.org

TREVOR Project
Crisis Intervention & Suicide Prevention for LGBTQ for ages 13-24
1.866.488.7386
www.thetrevorproject.org

Veterans Crisis Line
1.800.273.8255 – 24/7 Crisis Line
www.veteranscrisisline.net

Support Groups and Resources

Children's Safety Network (CSN)
Prevention of Childhood Injuries and Violence
www.childrenssafetynetwork.org

Indian Health Service (IHS)
Federal Health Program for American Indians & Alaska Natives
www.ihs.gov

NASP Resources
Preventing Youth Suicide Tips for Parents and Educators
www.nasponline.org

National Council for Suicide Prevention (NCSP)
www.ncsponline.org

Stopbullying.gov
www.stopbullying.gov

Suicide Prevention Resource Center (SPRC)
General: www.sprc.org
States & Communities: www.sprc.org/states

Yellow Ribbon
Dedicated to Preventing Youth Suicides
www.yellowribbon.org

Youth Suicide Prevention School-Based Guide
theguide.fmhi.usf.edu

S.A.R.A. Suicide Awareness Requires Action
Search by name on Facebook

Made in the USA
Charleston, SC
14 July 2014